process doesn't go quite as smoothly as she expected.

Have upcoming travel plans after a long time at home? Make sure not to end up like Noel Santillan, the subject of David Kushner's story "Where the @#$% Am I?," who gets hopelessly lost in rural Iceland—and becomes a local celebrity in the process.

And if you or someone in your life has bravely served our country, Lori Volkman's "Operation Order to My Deployed Husband" may bring a knowing smile to your face. In her tongue-in-cheek letter, the military spouse and popular blogger pokes fun at the rigidity of life in the armed forces and demands that her husband return home to treat his burgeoning case of "military brain."

At the end of the day, great comedy makes us view the world around us with a sparkle in our eyes. The right joke can forge a friendship, elicit that giggle you love from a child or partner, and reveal the many ways that we share common experiences on this big, funny planet. Whether they're knee-slapping, rib-tickling, sidesplitting, or gut-busting, these jokes—and a little laughter—will do your body good.

—THE EDITORS OF *READER'S DIGEST*

Laughter
the Best
Medicine

Laughter
the Best
Medicine

The Funniest Jokes, Stories, and Cartoons
from *Reader's Digest*

Reader's Digest

New York/Montreal

A READER'S DIGEST BOOK
© **2023 Trusted Media Brands, Inc.**
44 South Broadway
White Plains, NY 10601

The credits that appear on page 208 are hereby made part of this copyright page.

Cover illustration: Samantha Primuth

ISBN 978-1-62145-871-5 (dated)
ISBN 978-1-62145-876-0 (undated)

Component numbers:
119300104S (dated)
119300106S (undated)

We are committed to both the quality of our products and the service we provide
to our customers. We value your comments, so please feel free to contact us at
TMBBookTeam@TrustedMediaBrands.com.

For more Reader's Digest products and information, visit our website:
www.rd.com (in the United States)
www.readersdigest.ca (in Canada)

Printed in China
1 3 5 7 9 10 8 6 4 2

Contents

A NOTE FROM THE EDITORS

A **laugh a day** keeps the doctor away, or at least that's how it feels when a great joke hits you square in the funny bone.

In this book, we have collected the latest and greatest jokes, humor stories, cartoons, and more from the pages of *Reader's Digest*—a publication that has been sharing smiles with its audience for more than 100 years. And with hundreds of laughs in store—from popular columns including Laughter the Best Medicine, All in a Day's Work, Life in These United States, and Humor in Uniform—we guarantee that you'll never miss a dose of prescription-strength humor.

Turn the page to discover hilarious true stories, punchy one-liners, and other gags submitted by readers, along with the wittiest tweets the internet has to offer and quotes, jokes, and essays by celebrated comedians and humorists. No matter the jokester holding the pen, however, you're sure to see much of yourself reflected in these witty takes on everyday life. We've included recent favorites that perfectly encapsulate the absurdities of the workplace, hilarious anecdotes that highlight the pitfalls of dining out, punny quips that explore the sillier side of language, and quick one-liners that are great for a laugh when you just need a pick-me-up.

Do you ever feel mystified by the latest gadget on the market promising to change life as we know it? In the riotous essay "Prowling for Dust Bunnies," *New York Times* bestselling author Mary Roach takes the tech plunge by introducing a Roomba robot vacuum into her household cleaning routine. Spoiler alert: The

JOKE
APPÉTIT

On vacation in Hawaii, my stepmom, Sandy, called a cafe to make reservations for 7 p.m. Checking her book, the cheery young hostess said, "I'm sorry, all we have is 6:45. Will that time work for you?"

"That's fine," Sandy told her.

"OK," the woman confirmed. "Just be advised you may have to wait 15 minutes for your table."

—KELLY FINNEGAN

It always irked my single mother that her grocery store didn't carry eggs in packages of six—just by the dozen. Then one day, her wish came true: She walked into the store and found fresh eggs in cartons of six.

"I was so excited," she told us later, "that I bought two!"

—THOMAS HASSMANN

Whoever decided how much space should exist between tables in cafes and restaurants has so obviously never met a butt before.

—@ALANNABENNETT

I like to remind my kids who's boss by putting a cherry tomato on top of their ice cream sundaes every once in a while.

—@AWESOME_TODD

Kids are finicky eaters. On the Facebook page My Kid Can't Eat This, parents share just how finicky their little food critics really are:

- "My kid can't eat onion rings because, although he loves onion rings, recently he learned that they contain onions."
- "After my kids watched the movie *Ratatouille* 658,098,764 times and asked me to make what they made 787,628 times, I spent several hours scouring the internet for the exact recipe from the movie and made it. And now they can't eat it because a rat didn't make it."
- "Because she asked for cheese and crackers, not crackers and cheese."
- "My kid can't eat corn unless I cut it off the cob. He's 27."

Here's the problem with fruit: It's inconsistent. Some apples are delicious; some taste bad. Sometimes blueberries are great; sometimes they are disgusting. You know what's the same every time? Doritos.

—@PUNISHED_PICNIC

In front of the grocery store, a bubbly Girl Scout stood beside a table full of cookies.

"Please buy some cookies!" she begged.

"How much do they cost?" I asked.

"They're $5 a box, except these two kinds, which are $6 a box."

Figuring there must be something special about the $6 varieties, I asked why.

"Well, these are gluten-free," the little girl replied.

"And the others?"

She beamed. "Oh, those are overpriced!"

—KATHRYN THAYER

As she finished her dinner, my stuffed granddaughter turned to her mother and declared, "Mom, you make hamburgers so good, you could work at McDonald's!"

—LINDA RAUCH

If you're getting serious about someone, check what number their toaster is set on, because that's what you're going to be living with.

—@WILLIAMADER

After Sunday school, my 3-year-old, Kolby, exclaimed, "I hate Jesus! Jesus is yucky!" I was mortified. Several minutes went by as we drove home and terrible thoughts filled my head. Where had we gone wrong?

Finally I said, "Tell me why you hate Jesus. He died on the cross for us." Kolby tilted his head, and a perplexed look spread across his little face. This is it, I thought. He's going to reveal why he feels this way.

"Cheez-Its, Mom! I hate Cheez-Its!"

—YVONNE RUFF

Wit & Wordplay: Hot Cross Puns

■

A new study finds that sausages are often linked to other sausages.

—@DONNI

My wife was going to make pancakes. Then she wasn't. Then she was. Then she wasn't. Then she was. Now it looks like she's just waffling.

—@KENTWGRAHAM

I switched all the labels on my wife's spices. I'm not in trouble yet, but the thyme is cumin.

—JUSTIN MITCHELL

I ordered venison stew at the diner. It was five bucks.

—STEPHEN CANOVA

Support group for first pancakes

When our tour group entered a cafeteria for breakfast, the woman walking in with me made a beeline for the carrot cake. But just as she reached for a slice, she thought better of it and withdrew her hand. As she turned away, I heard her murmur, "No, it's too early for vegetables."

—BETTY ROSIAN

A Maryland man spent a year eating foods past their expiration dates—including moldy butter—to prove that those dates are arbitrary. *The Week* asked its readers to think of titles for an outdated foods cookbook. Here are the most (or least) appetizing submissions:

- *Green Eggs and Ham and Cheese and Salami*
- *Eat. Pray. Live?*
- *Pasta Its Prima*
- *Gone Appétit*

My granddaughter's life philosophy, which she quoted in a third grade essay: "Money can't buy happiness, but it can buy cows. Cows can make milk, and milk can make ice cream, and ice cream can make you happy."

—JOELLEN TURNER

A mother asks her young sons what they want for breakfast. The first little boy says, "I'll have some @#$%^& pancakes." The mother angrily sends him to his room for cursing. She then turns to the other little boy and, practically daring him, asks, "What do *you* want for breakfast?!" The second boy responds, "Well, I sure don't want the @#$%^& pancakes!"

—FREE-FUNNY-JOKES .COM

Recipes used to be terse instructions handwritten on an index card. Now you scroll through a Paris engagement story before you get to how to make the soup.

—@LIZHACKETT

This hot fudge sundae hasn't killed me, so it must be making me stronger.

—@ONLYFASTEDDIE

Like all growing boys, my teenage grandson, Jermon, was constantly hungry. I went to my refrigerator to find something he might like to eat. After poking around a bit and moving the milk and juice cartons, I spotted a bowl of leftover chili.

"Hey, Jermon," I called out excitedly. He came running into the kitchen. "Look! I found some chili."

Struggling to be polite, he said, "If you're that surprised, I'm not really sure I want it."

—MARILOU FLORES

I **stopped off** at the supermarket to buy my son-in-law his favorite pie, sour cream raisin. The box had the $15 price stamped on the top, which I thought would be tacky on a gift, so I asked the man behind the counter for a marker to black out the price. It didn't work—you could still see the price peeking through the dark ink.

"I know what to do," the man said. "This will cover it up."

And with that, he slapped a sticker over the price that read "$2.98 Day Old."

—MARGE DONNELL

A **customer came** to the counter and wanted to buy a Big Mac. When I told her we didn't have those, she asked for a Whopper instead. I told her we didn't have those either, and she got mad at me and walked away. I work at KFC.

—PLEASEFIREME
.TUMBLR.COM

M **y mother** was in a bakery and noticed a fly in the display case. The clerk must have noticed her look of dismay because she assured Mom, "Don't worry. They don't eat much."

—W.E.

A **fter our** meal at the pancake house, the waitress asked if we needed anything else.

"Yes," I said. "Could I get some more ice water, please?"

"Sure," she said. She then picked up my friend's glass of water, poured half into mine, and walked away.

—RICHARD HORNER

I **was standing** in a long lunch line with my husband when the guy in front of us looked down at my clearly pregnant belly, smiled, and asked, "What are you having?"

My very impatient husband curtly replied, "A steak sandwich."

—KAYLEN WADE

D **uring dinner,** I asked my 3-year-old granddaughter if her meal was good. She picked over the plate and thought for a moment before answering, "Not yet."

—WILLIAM YANNEY

Bought quick oats, then my roommate showed up with instant oats. I will not be humiliated; I must find an even sooner oat.
—@CHRISTHAYERSAYS

"Here's the wine you mispronounced."

At the supermarket, a customer buying a lot of groceries was checking out. As the clerk lifted the final bag, its bottom gave way, sending the contents crashing to the floor.

"They don't make these bags like they used to," the clerk said to the customer. "That was supposed to happen in your driveway."

—GCFL.NET

For Martin Luther King Day, I asked my fifth graders how they'd make the world a better place. One said, "I'd make potato skins a main dish rather than an appetizer."

—JESSICA CASTRONOVO

A man placed a package of cookies on my supermarket checkout counter. Unfortunately, one end of the package opened and most of the cookies came tumbling out.

"That was the last package!" he said.

"It's all right. We can give you a store credit," I assured him.

"No, I'll take these," he said, picking up the stray treats to repack them. "I promised my donkey cookies, and I can't go home without them."

—JOHN FLYNN

A VERY CIVIL WAR

One transplanted gentleman explains
the ins and outs of the South's tricky gentility.

By Roy Blount Jr.

Come on in! Busy? Me? No! Sit right down here in my favorite chair and keep me up all night and drink all my liquor. Can I run out and kill our last chicken and fry her up for you? No? Wouldn't take a minute. Are you sure? Oh, don't let the chicken hear you. She'll be so disappointed.

What can I do to make you comfortable here?

You want me to tell you about Southern hospitality?

Well.

It is true that I have long lived largely in the North but am Southern. So I have a certain perspective. I have never gotten over the sight of whatever it was that was served to me as fried chicken one night in Akron.

"This is fried chicken?" I asked the waiter. He looked at it. "I think so," he said. I rest my case. But that doesn't mean there is no such thing as Northern hospitality. True, it is possible to meet with a less than heartwarming reception up north.

I remember one Sunday morning in Cambridge, Massachusetts. I went to a cafeteria to get coffee and a doughnut before meeting a friend.

I took a ticket from a ticket machine, then ordered from the woman behind the steam table, who was gazing with angst down into a vat of scrambled eggs. I was tempted to tell her I agreed that scrambled eggs should never be assembled in vat-size proportions, but she seemed to be thinking about something even worse. Without speaking or even looking up, she served me and punched my ticket to show how much I owed. I then presented the ticket to the woman standing at the cash register.

Everything seemed to be in order.

I wasn't expecting anything more than a smooth transaction, but I was admittedly expecting that—a smooth transaction.

The woman at the cash register looked at my ticket, then raised her eyes as though in supplication.

"Jaysus Murray and Jeosuph," she cried, pursing her lips unevenly like Humphrey Bogart. "Why do all you people come in on weekends?"

That was 50 years ago. To this day, I don't know what was wrong.

But I wouldn't call that an example of Northern hospitality, exclusively.

In Nashville, Tennessee, I cultivated a hamburger joint for weeks, ordering the same thing every time. Finally, I came in and said, "The usual."

"You mean 'the regular,'" the counter person, named Opaline, said.

I thought I meant "the usual." I thought I was the regular. But I wasn't going to argue with Opaline.

"The regular, then," I said.

"In your case," she said, "what's that, exactly?"

Still, Southern hospitality is an institution. Before air conditioning, climate was a major factor. In the South, people were more likely to be sitting out on the porch when folks showed up. You couldn't pretend not to be home when there you were, sitting on the porch. You could pretend to be dead, but then you couldn't fan yourself.

"This is fried chicken?" I asked the waiter. "I think so," he said.

Even today, rhetoric is a factor. The salesperson in Atlanta may give you just as glazed a look as the one in Boston. But the former is more likely to say, "These overalls are going to make your young one look cute as a doodlebug's butt." Southerners still derive energy from these figures of speech, just as plants do from photosynthesis.

Northern hospitality can be summed up thusly: You walk into a dry cleaner's for the 30th time, and the proprietor, recognizing you at long last, says, "You again!" If you are willing to accept that he is never going to welcome you, then you're welcome. The advantage of this form of Northern hospitality is that it works irritation right into the equation, up front. Let's face it: People tend to irritate one another. Especially hosts and guests.

Irritation is a part of Southern hospitality too. Say you run into a Southerner where you live in the North. And you take a thorn out of his paw or something, and he declares, "I want you to come visit us! And sleep in my bed! Me and Mama will take the cot! And bring your whole family with you!"

"Yes, do come," says the Southern wife. "We would love it."

"And I want you to hold my little baby daughter on your lap!" her husband cries. "And Mama will cook up a whole lot of groceries, and we'll all eat ourselves half to death!"

And sure enough, you take them up on the invitation and show up. And the Southerners swing wide the portal, blink a little, and then recognize you and start hollering, "You came! Hallelujah! Sit down here! How long can you stay? Oh no, you got to stay longer than a week; it'll take that long just to eat the old milk cow. Junior, run out back and kill Louisa. Milk her first.

"Here, let us carry all your bags—oh, isn't this a nice trunk—upstairs and then..."

You are a little disappointed to note that there is no veranda.

"Oh, we lost our veranda in the Waw. Which Waw? Why, the Waw with you all. But that's all right."

And you are prevailed upon to stay a couple of weeks, and you yield to the Southerners' insistence that you eat three huge meals a day and several snacks to "tide you over"—and finally you override the Southerners' pleas that you stay around till the scuppernongs get ripe, and they say "Well, I guess if you got your heart set on running off and leaving us" in a put-out tone of voice, and they pack up a big lunch of homemade pecan pie and collard greens for you to eat on the way home, and after you go through about an hour and a half of waving and repeating that you really do have to go and promising to come back, soon, and to bring more relatives next time, you go back north.

And the Southerners close their door. And they slump back up against it. And they look at each other wide-eyed. And they say, shaking their heads over the simplemindedness of Yankees, "They came!"

"And like to never left!"

"And ate us out of house and home!"

My husband was displeased with the jar of pimiento-stuffed green olives he had bought: "They're just not vinegary."

"They were vinegary when I ate them," said our youngest son.

"When did you eat them?" I asked.

"Just this morning. I sucked all the red things out and put the olives back in the jar."

—LINDA BENNETT

The best way to prepare cauliflower is by throwing it in the trash while ordering a delicious pizza.

—@NICKYOUSSEF

I wanted to go out tonight, but the avocado I bought will finally be ripe enough to eat between 8 p.m. and 8:15 p.m., so I can't.

—@TANISHALOVE

Waiters will tell you there's always one customer who sticks out. Here are some particularly memorable examples:

- "A customer returned a baked potato because it 'looked like it was dug out of the ground.'"
- "I had a guest ask me for a 'gluten-free wheat beer.'"
- "A customer wanted 'canned Coke' ... but in a bottle."
- "I worked for a restaurant that served Polynesian sauce. One man would always come in and ask for 'Pomeranian' sauce. No one ever corrected him."

—BUZZFEED.COM

Farmer McDonald set up a roadside stand to sell his fresh vegetables, and a very curious customer asked McDonald if his tomatoes were genetically modified.

"No, not at all," said the tomatoes.

—THEIRISHGIFTHOUSE .COM

The sum of the cabbage is directly proportional to the square root of the carrot divided by the mayo. That is Cole's Law.

—@SUADSHAMMA

Over dinner, I explained the health benefits of a colorful meal to my family. "The more colors, the more variety of nutrients," I told them. Pointing to our food, I asked, "How many different colors do you see?" "Six," volunteered my daughter. "Seven if you count the burned parts."

—ALLISON BEVANS

Scene: a morning with my 6-year-old granddaughter, Emma.

Me: Would you like bacon and eggs for breakfast?

Emma: I only like eggs when they're mixed with something.

Me: Like omelets?

Emma: No, like fudge brownies.

—ELIZABETH COOPER

What's it called when eating something exceptionally spicy makes you feel exceptionally ill? The editors of *The Week* were wondering just that after a New York man who scarfed down a superhot Carolina Reaper chili pepper was rushed to the hospital. The magazine's clever readers coined these pseudomedical terms:
- Jalepaiño
- Fire-arrhea
- Hellitosis
- Habañeurosis
- Endoblasty
- Roastacea
- Firebromyalgia
- Scarlet pepper fever
- Incendiary bowel syndrome

My freshman year of college, my grandma mailed me a batch of sugar cookies for my birthday but wrote in the card that she'd put jalapeños in them. This was so that I would know she was thinking of me "but wouldn't gain the weight."

—THECHIVE.COM

Tired of boiling water every time you make pasta? Boil a few gallons at the beginning of the week and freeze it for later.

—@SWAGLORDPAT

Let's Talk Turkey

■

My wife got a free-range, organic, non-GMO, antibiotic-free turkey this year—and every one of those adjectives added 20 bucks.

—@KENTWGRAHAM

Most turkeys taste better the day after. My mother's tasted better the day before.

—RITA RUDNER

If you're ever feeling down on yourself, just remember how in 2018, when I hosted Thanksgiving for my family, I told them to park in the wrong spot and every single person's car got towed.

—@DXXNYA

I dropped my ice cream cone on the ground, and it landed pointy end up, which made the earth, at least for a moment, one giant topping.

—@BRIANBOWMAN73

Grateful to the visionary who saw beans that had been fried only one time and thought "This isn't enough."

—@GINNYHOGAN

Just burned 2,000 calories. That's the last time I leave brownies in the oven while I nap.

—@YIKYAKAPP

Our manager kept reminding us waitresses to encourage customers to order dessert. At the end of an especially tiring day, I walked over to a couple who had just sat down, gave them each a menu and a glass of water, and asked, "Would you care for anything else?"

—JUNE WARBURTON

After ordering a sandwich at a deli, I remembered I wanted to split it with my wife, so I asked the clerk to cut it in fourths. "Too late," he said, handing me the sandwich. "I already cut it in half."

—RODNEY BISHOP

"Got anything else? I gave up carbs."

When my dad, a good ol' boy from the South, visited me in Manhattan, I treated him to dinner at an elegant French restaurant. Since he was out of his element, I ordered for him, choosing the beef bourguignon with a side of polenta, which he loved. That night, I overheard him on the phone with my stepmother.

"Dinner was great," he raved. "But you won't believe how much they charge here for pot roast and grits."

—JULIE WEHMEYER

My husband and I both work, so our family eats out a lot. Recently, when we were having a rare home-cooked meal, I handed a glass to my 3-year-old and told her to drink her milk. She looked at me bewildered and replied, "But I didn't order milk."

—JANET A. NUSSBAUM

Rummaging through my elderly mother's freezer, I found pierogi and offered to cook them for her. "No," she said. "Your sister made them, but I don't like pierogi." "Did you tell her that?" I asked. "Of course not," she said, scoffing at the very idea. "If I did, she wouldn't bring them anymore."

—DAVE CURRAN

Occasionally at the restaurant where I work there are extra desserts, and the staff are given some to take home. Once I brought home two pieces of cheesecake for my son and daughter. Katie had a piece that evening. The next day her older brother found her watching TV and eating more cheesecake.

"Are you eating my cheesecake right now?" he demanded.

"Oh, no," she replied sweetly, "I ate your piece yesterday."

—BRENDA GINGRICH

For Lent, I gave up ice cream, fast food, and pizza, but obviously not lying.

—DOUG TORKELSON

The first stage of a realistic baking show would be each contestant trying to open a jammed utensil drawer.

—@BLADE_FUNNER

Accidentally went grocery shopping on an empty stomach, and now I'm the proud owner of aisle seven.

—@DOMESTICGODDSS

I once had a customer ask that his lamb not taste like lamb.

—REDDIT.COM

I hate cooking, but I am excited to debut my cookbook *Toast on a Paper Towel, 365 Ways.*

—@LIZHACKETT

Our teenage granddaughter was thrilled when she landed her first real job waiting tables. But after one shift, the excitement seemed to have waned.

"How do you like being a waitress?" I asked her.

She shrugged, "It would be OK if people wouldn't keep asking for stuff."

—CHARLES FINLON

Starving after hours of driving nonstop, my husband and I pulled over at a truck stop. While he gassed up the car, I went into the restaurant and placed our order to go. After writing it all down, the girl behind the register asked, "Will that be all for you?"

"No," I replied a bit defensively. "Some of it's for my husband."

—JANET HULL

I was new to the South when I stopped off at a fast-food restaurant. When my order arrived, I pointed out that the dressing on the salad was orange rather than the ranch I had requested.

"Oh, sorry, hon," the clerk replied. "You said *ranch*. I thought you said *Franch*."

—DEBRA GRIZZLE

A man's bragging about his recent promotion to vice president got so out of hand that even his wife was annoyed.

"Look, being a vice president isn't that special," she said. "They even have a vice president of peas at the supermarket!"

Not believing her for one second, the man called the supermarket and demanded, "Get me the vice president of peas!"

The clerk replied, "Fresh, canned, or frozen?"

—NORMAN MIDDLETON

I was sprawled on the living room couch watching my favorite show on the Food Network when my husband walked in.

"Why do you watch those food shows?" he asked. "You don't even cook."

Glaring back at him, I asked, "Then why do you watch football?"

—LINDSAY WRIGHT

Once heard a guy climbed Everest "because it was there" and just feel like the reason for one of the most strenuous feats in existence should be different than the reason I ate an entire gallon of ice cream.

—@THEANDREWNADEAU

"Your security clearance isn't high enough to order any of the dishes made from the chef's secret recipes."

A LOT OF PEOPLE GET A RECORD DEAL AND SPEND THAT MONEY ON STUFF. I SPENT IT ON CHEESE, BASICALLY.
—SAM SMITH

Karma's going to make sure I come back as a lobster—I've cooked too many.
—DAVID CHANG

Be nice to everyone and make your own cup of tea on set.
—SAOIRSE RONAN

Hard work should be rewarded by good food.
—KEN FOLLETT

Happiness is an egg salad sandwich with the salt, pepper, and mayo in exactly the right proportion.
—EUGENE LEVY

I'm not a vegetarian because I love animals. I'm a vegetarian because I hate plants.
—A. WHITNEY BROWN

Large, naked, raw carrots are acceptable as food only to those who live in hutches eagerly awaiting Easter.
—FRAN LEBOWITZ

Man cannot live by coffee alone, but he will give it a good try.
—HARRY STYLES

Vegetables are a must on a diet. I suggest carrot cake, zucchini bread, and pumpkin pie.
—JIM DAVIS

YOU CAN TAKE A GIRL OUT OF THE MIDWEST BUT DON'T COME FOR HER BABY BACK RIBS.
—SHONDA RHIMES

AMISH FRIENDSHIP BREAD

When it came to this "share if you dare" starter, it was every woman for herself!

By Ann Morrow

Recently, I opened the front door to a friend's frantic knocking. Holding up a bowl, she said, *"Please* take it."

"What is it?" I asked, concerned.

"Amish friendship bread. And you have to follow the rules."

Bread rules?

"Keep it at room temperature. Don't put the lid on too tight. Stir for the first five days. On Day Five, add 1 cup each of milk, flour, and sugar. Stir for four more days."

I grabbed a pen and started writing.

"On Day Ten, feed it again. Keep 1 cup for yourself, then divide the rest and give it to three friends."

As she ran back to her car, she yelled, "But don't bring any to me!"

I lifted the lid and promptly got a whiff of pure sewer gas. I snapped it shut and shoved it behind the toaster.

On Day Two, when I remembered to stir, the starter had ruptured the Tupperware lid, and smelly globs had bubbled onto the countertop. Great.

On Day Five, I fed the thing. That night I woke with a start, sensing something was wrong. I tiptoed to the kitchen. My stinky countertop companion had erupted yet again and was making for the front door. I spent the rest of the evening scraping it into an ice cream bucket.

For the next 96 hours, I dared not leave the house. On the hour, I warily stirred, carefully keeping the cat away lest he be swallowed whole.

By daybreak of Day Ten, I was dividing the mix into bowls and then speeding down the road in search of unsuspecting friends. An end in sight!

But as I arrived home, I spotted a dish on my doorstep. A note read, "I offer you this starter batch of Amish friendship bread. Enjoy!"

WHAT
A TRIP

Traveling through the Midwest, I stopped at an Ohio welcome center to pick up a state map. I found plenty of brochures but no maps. Then I spotted two employees and asked whether they had any available.

"Sure," said the first guy. "I'll get you one."

As he walked to the back, the second guy explained, "We keep them in the storage room. If we leave them out on the counter, people just come in and take them."

—JAMES NEALIS

Before our trip to Las Vegas, my husband lost quite a few pounds. This came into play on the airplane. As he was grabbing our overhead luggage, his pants slipped down to his knees. A woman asked, "Can I help you?"

"Yes," he said. "I'll grab the luggage; you pull up my pants."

—JEANNE GELMER

Stormy weather diverted our Dallas-bound flight to another airport. As we approached the runway, the pilot came on the intercom: "For those of you who are not familiar with the area, this is Lubbock, Texas." Then he paused. "And for those of you who *are* familiar with this area, I *think* this is Lubbock, Texas."

—DARRELL BURTON

As Canadians living in Miami, we often drove back to Canada for vacations. One year we decided to drive up for the Christmas holidays. When we reached the border, the customs official took one look at our Florida license plates and said, "Anyone dumb enough to leave Florida this time of year can't be smart enough to smuggle anything. Go on through!"

—MRS. M. T. SMITH

My wife takes 13 bikinis for a four-day beach trip. Meanwhile, I'm rocking the swimming trunks my mom bought at Kmart in 1991.

—@BIGHEB7

On our way to go spelunking, we got lost on a country road. We stopped to ask a farmer, "Is this the road to Waynesville?" "Yes, it is," he replied. As we started to drive away, we barely heard him add, "But you're going the wrong way."
—DOUG HISSONG

After many trips over the years to Disney World with our nephew, my husband and I were eager to hear about his first time there without us and on his own dime. He summed it up quite well when he said, "I discovered that Disney World is not so magical when I'm the one who's paying for it."

—BARBARA ANDREWS

On a fishing trip to a remote lake in northern Quebec, I asked the outfitter, "Do you stay here during the winter?"

"No," he said. "The snow gets too deep. We can't get supplies in. Like many Canadians, I go south for the winter."

"Oh," I said. "Where do you go?"

"Vermont."

—DAVID RICHARDSON

A jet ran into some turbulent weather. To help the passengers remain calm, the flight attendants brought out the beverage carts.

"I'd like a soda," said a passenger in the first row. Moving along, the attendant asked the man behind her if he would like something.

"Yes, I would," he replied. "Give me whatever the pilot is drinking!"

—MARY J. MILLER

When the fellow called a motel and asked how much they charged for a room, the clerk told him that the rates depended on room size and number of people.

"Do you take kids?" the man asked.

"No, sir," replied the clerk. "Only cash and credit cards."

—SUCCESSFUL MEETINGS MAGAZINE

I've noticed that fewer drivers are using their turn signals, and it makes me crazy. I was with a friend who wasn't using his directional, and I asked why. He shot back, "You know what? It's nobody's business which direction I'm turning!"

—NPR.ORG

As I waited for my luggage at the airport, a man lifted my suitcase off the baggage carousel.

"Excuse me, sir!" I shouted, trying to get his attention. "That's my suitcase you've got there."

The man shot back defensively, "Well, somebody took mine!"

—C.S.

My husband and I were relaxing on lounge chairs on a Jamaica beach, half listening to a couple walking ankle deep in the clear water. The woman was extolling the beauty of the island when suddenly she let out a scream.

"Oh!" she shrieked. "There are fish in here!"

—JANET DAVIS

"I guess we'll never know why they beach themselves."

"**Was Grandpa** mad when they went through his luggage at the border?"

"No, not in the least. They found the pair of glasses he'd lost two weeks earlier."

—MIKLOS MADARASZ

After a visit to Yellowstone's Old Faithful, our family stopped at a gas station outside of the park. Our daughter leaned over a water fountain, and just as she was about to take a sip, the water shot up and sprayed her face. The gas station attendant smiled and said, "That's why we call it Old Faceful."

—SHARRON NELSON WOOD

My son took his first flight at the age of 4. He was scared about flying, so he called the attendant over and told her that he wanted the plane not to "flight" but just to get "going on the road!" The flight attendant played along and agreed. As the plane sped down the runway, my son called back to her, "I told you by road, but not so fast!!!"

—ANA CAROLINA CARRILLO

I think my pilot was a little inexperienced. We were sitting on the runway, and he said, "OK, folks, we're gonna be taking off in just a few—*whoa!* Here we go."

—KEVIN NEALON

Before heading off to Mexico on vacation, my daughter asked her doctor for medicine to ward off any potential stomach troubles. Instead, the doctor prescribed bottled water and electrolytes, "which have simple sugars and salt." My daughter liked the sound of that.

"Oh," she said, "like a margarita?"

—KAARYN ROBERTS

After my husband and I were married, my in-laws offered to pay for our honeymoon. Visions of Hawaii or Mexico came to mind. Not quite. They told us we were heading to Disney World. Not only that, but since they'd always wanted to go, they were coming along. Turns out, my mother-in-law's two best friends also always wanted to go to Disney World, as did their three kids, not to mention my sister-in-law and her

husband. I can't say a lot of honeymooning went on.

—CRISTINA BEITZ

While sightseeing in Kentucky, we stopped to take a tour of Mammoth Cave. A visitor in our group,

looking up at the huge domed ceiling, asked the guide, "Has there ever been a cave-in?"

"Never," the guide reassured us. "But if there was, look on the bright side. Where else could you get buried for $2.50?"

—DOUGLAS MAXSON

No Stupid Questions
■

Our tour guide at historic Arlington National Cemetery thought he had an answer for everything ... until he met our students. "Excuse me," said one kid. "Are the graves in alphabetical order?"
—WILLIAM CULLEM

When I was a tour guide at Niagara Falls, the most common question was "What time do they turn the water off?"
—@CHRISDOBMEIER

A customer called our Los Angeles travel agency asking how much a round-trip flight to Hawaii would cost. Evidently, she didn't care for the price I quoted her, because the next thing she asked was, "How far is it if we decide to drive?"
—GLORIA MELVILLE

WHERE THE @#$% AM I?

He wanted an adventure.
Thanks to his confused GPS, he got one.

By **David Kushner**

Before Noel Santillan became famous for getting lost in Iceland, he was just another guy from New Jersey looking for adventure armed with the modern traveler's two essentials: a dream and, more important, a GPS unit.

On a frigid, dark February morning in 2016, the 28-year-old Sam's Club marketing manager was driving away from Keflavík International Airport in a rented Nissan hatchback toward a hotel in Reykjavík, about 40 minutes away. He was excited that his one-week journey was beginning but groggy from the five-hour red-eye flight. As the sun rose over the ocean and illuminated the snow-covered lava rocks along the shore, Santillan dutifully followed the commands of the GPS that came with the car, a calm female voice directing him to an address on Laugarvegur Road— a left here, a right there.

But after stopping on a desolate gravel road next to a sign for a gas station, Santillan got the feeling that the voice might be steering him wrong. He'd already been driving for nearly an hour, yet the ETA on the GPS put his arrival time at around 5:20 p.m., eight hours later. He reentered his destination and got the same result. Though he sensed that something was off, he decided to trust the machine.

The farther he drove, the fewer cars he saw. The roads became icier. The only stations he could find on the radio were airing talk shows in Icelandic. He hadn't set up his phone for international use, so that was no help. At around 2 p.m., as his tires skidded along a narrow mountain road that skirted a steep cliff, he knew that the device had failed him.

He was lost and—despite the calm insistence of his GPS—nowhere near his hotel. There were no other drivers on the road, and there was little else to do but follow the line on the screen to its mysterious end. "I knew I was going to get somewhere," he says. "I didn't know where else to go."

The directions ended at a small blue house in a tiny town. A woman answered his knock. She smiled as he stammered about his hotel and handed her his reservation.

No, she told him, this wasn't his hotel, and he wasn't in Reykjavík. That city was 225 miles south. He was in Siglufjördhur, a fishing village of 1,300 people on the northern coast. The woman, whose name happened to be Sirry—pronounced just like the Apple bot that offers users directions through life—quickly figured out what had happened. The address on Expedia (and his reservation printout) was wrong. The hotel was on Laugavegur, but Expedia had accidentally spelled the street name with an extra r—Laugarvegur.

Santillan checked in to a local hotel to get some sleep, with the plan of driving to Reykjavík the next day. When he told his story to the woman at the front desk, she chuckled. "I'm sorry. I shouldn't laugh at this," she said, "but it's just too funny."

The next morning, when he went to check out, the joke continued.

"Some reporters want to talk with you," said the hotel receptionist.

Sirry had posted his absurd story on her Facebook page, and it had quickly been shared around. A Facebook friend of hers, the editor of an Icelandic travel site, wrote a blog post on the "extraordinary and funny incident." Soon his misadventure had attracted the interest of TV and radio journalists.

Santillan sensed something was off but decided to trust the machine.

They weren't the only ones who wanted to talk with Santillan.

"Everybody in the town knew about me," he says. Some Siglufjördhurians came to the hotel to welcome him and take pictures. One offered him a tour of the village's pride and joy, the Icelandic Herring Era Museum. The chef at Santillan's hotel prepared the local beef stew for him, on the house.

Enjoying all the hospitality, Santillan decided to spend an extra night. The following day, he went on TV, explaining to a reporter that he'd always found GPS to be so reliable in the past. By the time he made it to Reykjavík that evening, he had become a full-blown sensation in the national media, which dubbed him the Lost Tourist. *DV*, an Icelandic tabloid, marveled that despite all the warning signs, the American had "decided to trust the [GPS]." Before long, his experience made

international news, with coverage on the BBC and in the *New York Times*. The manager of the hotel in Reykjavík had seen reports on his odyssey and offered him a free stay and a meal at the fish restaurant next door.

Out in the streets, which were full of revelers celebrating the annual Winter Lights Festival, Icelanders corralled the Lost Tourist for selfies and plied him with shots of the local poison, Brennivín, an unsweetened schnapps. As a band played a rock song outside, Santillan kept hearing people shouting his name. Some guys dragged him up a stairway to a strip club, where one of the dancers also knew his name. The whole thing seemed surreal. "I just felt like, This isn't happening to me," he says.

Still, he was going to ride it out as long as he could. After the marketing manager of the country's most famous getaway, the Blue Lagoon geothermal spa, wrote him offering a free visit, Santillan headed there the next day. The address came preloaded in his rental car's GPS, since it was the one place everyone wanted to go.

As Santillan drove out under the winter sky, he marveled at how far he had come. He pictured himself resting in the cobalt blue waters, breathing in the steam. But half an hour later, when his GPS told him he had arrived, he got a sinking feeling. Looking out the window, he saw no signs of a geothermal spa, just a small lone building in what seemed like the middle of nowhere. The Lost Tourist was lost again.

For whatever reason, the GPS had led him not to the Blue Lagoon but to some convention center off an empty road. As he stepped into the building, he was recognized. The fact that Santillan was lost again made him all the more credible. After patiently posing for a bunch of pictures, he succumbed to an old-fashioned way of getting to where he was going: following the directions given to him by another human being.

And so, with the GPS turned off, he drove on—a right here, a left there—looking for landmarks along the way. Before long, he was soaking in a steamy bath, white volcanic mud smeared on his face. By then he'd already vowed to return to Iceland. Maybe, he thought, I'll even live here at some point.

Until he returns, he has something to remember his misadventure by: an Icelandic GPS. The rental agency presented it to him when he returned his Nissan. It's a reminder of his time as the Lost Tourist, a nickname he considers a badge of honor. "I like it," he says. "If you don't lose yourself, you're never going to find yourself."

"I told you the tank was half-empty, but oh no, you said it was half-full."

"Aaahhhhhh!!"

That was my sister's way of letting the whole world know that she'd just seen a mouse inside her Adirondack Mountains cabin. Her husband set a trap to catch the uninvited guest, and later that night they heard it suddenly snap shut.

As my brother-in-law carried the trap to the garbage, my sister scrutinized the little beast, then shook her head in frustration.

"No," she said, "that's not him."

—PATRICIA CHESTER

Wit & Wordplay: Foreign Language Foibles

■

After I paid for my items in an adorable Italian shop, the salesperson smiled and said *"grazie,"* Italian for "thank you." My Italian isn't very good, but I knew that the Italian word for "you're welcome" was the same as the name of a spaghetti sauce. So I confidently replied *"Ragú!"* and walked out of the store. A few blocks later, it hit me: I had the wrong spaghetti sauce. "You're welcome" is *prego*.

—THERESA TURCOTTE

While visiting Spain, a friend of mine became embarrassed about something and let the entire bar know by shouting *"Estoy muy embarazada! Estoy muy embarazada!"* Soon, she was even more embarrassed. *Embarazada* means *"pregnant."*

—FLUENCYCORP.COM

An American couple visiting in a German village stepped into a small shop to look for souvenirs. The woman sneezed. *"Gesundheit!"* said the clerk. "Charles," the American woman said to her husband, "we're in luck. There's somebody here who speaks English."

—OHIO MOTORIST

An elderly woman was nervous about making her first flight in an airplane, so before takeoff she went to speak to the captain about her fears.

"You will bring me down safely, won't you?" she anxiously inquired.

"There's no need to worry, madam," was his friendly reply. "I haven't left anyone up there yet."

—COLLEEN BURGER

The best time to go to Disney World, if you want to avoid huge crowds, is 1962.

—DAVE BARRY

Kanin

"It says the cost of the flight went up because we acknowledged its existence."

Since it was my first time in a Las Vegas casino, I asked an employee to walk me through how the slot machines worked. He showed me how to insert a bill, hit the spin button, and operate and release the handle. "And where does the money come out?" I asked. He pointed to a far wall. "From that ATM, most of the time."

—JAY JANI

Good thing most planes have TVs. Nothing's worse than having to look out the window at Earth's sacred majesty from the point of view of angels.

—@PHARMASEAN

In a panic, a traveler called down to the hotel's front desk soon after checking in.

"Help!" he yelled. "I'm trapped inside my room!"

"What do you mean, trapped?" the front desk attendant asked.

"Well, I see three doors," the man explained. "The first opens to a closet, and the second to a bathroom. And the third door has a Do Not Disturb sign hanging on it."

—PETER S. GREENBERG

Heading into the jungle on his first safari, the American visitor was confident he could handle any emergency. He sidled up to the experienced local guide and said smugly, "I know that carrying a torch will keep lions away."

"True," the guide replied. "But it depends on how fast you carry the torch."

—E.H.

Traveling through Spain, my friend Amy and I soaked in the culture, gorged ourselves on excellent food, and basically indulged our every whim. One day we walked into a shop that had the most gorgeous coats. As we tried a few on, we noticed the odd looks we were getting from the shopkeepers. We didn't know why until one kind English-speaking patron took pity on us.

"Excuse me," she said, a small smile forming on her face. "This is a dry cleaners."

—ROSIE SPIEGEL

Airport security confiscated my Bengay. They accused me of packing heat.

—DAVE WEINBAUM

AIRBNB REVIEWS FROM FICTION LAND

Some imaginary destinations deserve five-star ratings. Most of them don't.

By Andy Simmons

*T*he **most** memorable vacations often seem too good to be true. For the following travelers, they actually were.

TARA
Clayton County, Georgia
Hostess: Scarlett O'Hara

REVIEWS

Elizabeth: On our very first morning, the proprietress, a Miss Scarlett, barged into our room, ripped down the curtains, and said, "I'm going to a party, and I need a dress." With the sun streaming in through the windows, we didn't get much sleep after that.

Dean: The next morning, Miss Scarlett ripped the comforter off our bed, yelling, "I'm getting married! I need a wedding dress!" Honestly! I yelled out to her, "What are you going to take tomorrow?!" She shrugged and said, "Tomorrow is another day." Well, not for us. We packed our bags and found a lovely room over at the Wilkeses', not far away.

HAY, STICK, AND BRICK HOUSES
Third Pigsty on the Right
Hosts: The Three Little Pigs

REVIEWS

Louis: Every morning we awoke to the same racket—their neighbor shouting "Little pig, little pig, let me come in." One of the pigs would yell back something about chinny chin chins, and the next thing we knew, the whole house came down around us, which was very embarrassing because I sleep in my underwear.

Tim: I'm deathly allergic to hay, so as far as I'm concerned, the wolf actually did me a favor blowing down the house.

Response from Hosts: Louis, Tim, please know we've patched things up with our neighbor, Mr. Wolf. We'd like to invite you back to enjoy a complimentary bowl of slop as well as a free night in our brand-new underground cement-and-steel-fortified bunker. We think you'll find it even more durable than our brick design.

THE RED KEEP
King's Landing, Westeros
Hostess: Queen Cersei Lannister

REVIEWS

Ashley: We came to King's Landing because we'd heard something about a Game of Thrones, and my husband and I are competition addicts.

Marc: If you can get past the beheadings, poisonings, pillaging, and spotty Wi-Fi, then this is a fun place. I swear, after every battle, the wine flows and people make out. So much better than the Sandals Resort in Jamaica!

Jody: Queen Cersei was quite accommodating, loading us with pelts for our bed and booking us on adventure tours. I'd never laid siege to a city before! When I get home, I'm going to gather my Zumba class and see whether we can invade Dayton!

301 COBBLESTONE WAY
Town of Bedrock
Hosts: Fred and Wilma Flintstone

REVIEWS

Mitchell: I was so tired by the end of a busy day in Bedrock that I fell asleep the instant my head hit the pillow. That's because my pillow was made of schist and I was knocked unconscious. When my alarm clock tapped me on the shoulder eight hours later and told me—rather rudely, I thought—to wake up, I marched into Mr. Flintstone's kitchen and demanded a new pillow. Mr. Flintstone offered me a marble pillow from the Martha Stewart Home Collection, which I refused.

Ned: I applaud the Flintstones for being environmentally aware. They own a hybrid car powered by both right and left feet.

Ruth: I am so buying a woolly mammoth dishwasher!

"Dan, you forgot to put on your out-of-office."

My wife and I were driving from the subzero cold of our home in Wisconsin to a winter vacation in Arizona. During the long drive south, the weather was getting warmer and warmer. Eventually, the outside temperature was in the low 60s, and we felt hot. We marveled at how our bodies were so acclimated to the Wisconsin cold that this moderate temperature seemed so hot to us. In fact, we were feeling uncomfortably warm and thinking about putting on the air conditioner when suddenly my wife exclaimed, "Oh my gosh, the seat heaters are on!"

—**RANDY BERDAL**

Upon arriving at our beach-house rental, I noticed that it was filthy. So I grabbed the cleaning supplies and proceeded to scrub the toilets, floors, bathtubs, and kitchen cabinets. I was so upset that the house was not ready for guests. Later, my family and I discovered that we were supposed to be staying at the house next door. I had "white-gloved" the wrong place.

—**TANYA LELAND**

America's national parks are treasures to behold. Or at least most of us think so. Here are one-star Yelp reviews from tourists who beg to differ.

- *Sequoia:* "There are bugs and stuff, and they will bite you on your face."
- *Yellowstone:* "It's like a bigger version of Central Park, only with bears."
- *Yosemite:* "Trees block views, and too many gray rocks."
- *The Grand Canyon:* "A hole. A very, very large hole."
- *Isle Royale:* "No cell service and terrible Wi-Fi."
- *Arches:* "Narcissistic, selfish people posed right in front of the arch for their personal photo."
- *Denali:* "The bus stops way too much."

—BACKPACKERS.COM

Driving across California, we stopped at a red light in a beautiful old western town. As I admired the elegant storefronts and beautiful scenery, I didn't notice that the light had turned green and back to red again. It was then that a police officer tapped on my window and said, "That's all the colors we got here."

—YEFIM M. BRODD

Some people like to travel by train because it combines the slowness of a car with the cramped public exposure of an airplane.

—DENNIS MILLER

Low on gas while on a trip to Las Vegas, I pulled my van into a service station. As I was turning in, I spied lying on the ground a gas cap that looked like it might replace my missing one. I hurriedly parked by the pump, jumped out of the van, ran over, and picked up the stray cap. I was pleasantly surprised to find that it screwed easily onto my tank.

What a perfect fit, I thought. And then I noticed the keyhole in the top of the cap.

—BOB SJOSTRAND

Fun tip: Instead of going on vacation with a baby, stand outside until you're sunburned, then light $1,000 on fire.

—@JULIUSSHARPE

A late arrival at the Nashville airport left me in front of a car rental agent one night. In a heavy southern drawl, she asked, "Can Ah help y'all?" After processing my order, she said, "I have an accent. Is that OK?" "I don't mind at all," I said. "Being from New England, I have one too." She waited a minute before replying, "I meant the car. I have a Hyundai Accent."

—JOSEPH FERRI

When my daughter Rhonda was little, we took a family vacation to Florida. We were seated on the airplane near the wing, and I pointed out to her that we were flying above the ocean.

"Can you see the water?" I asked.

"No," Rhonda said, peering out the window at the wing, "but I can see the diving board."

—REBECCA RICCI

While visiting Yellowstone National Park some years back, my friend and I met with a ranger who was in charge of maintaining order in the campsites. He showed us how to operate the new garbage cans; the complex models had a rotating upper section and a special door designed to keep out hungry bears. Impressed, I asked the ranger whether the fortified cans were working as intended. He shook his head with a smile.

"Not really," he said. "We're finding considerable overlap in the intelligence of the smartest bears and the dumbest campers."

—GUY NELSON

A Swiss man looking for directions pulls up at a bus stop in Zurich where two American tourists are waiting.

"*Entschuldigung, können Sie Deutsch sprechen?*" he asks.

The two Americans just stare at him.

"*Parlez-vous français?*" he tries.

The two Americans continue to stare.

"*Parlate italiano?*"

No response. The Swiss guy gives up and drives off. The first American turns to the second and says, "We should really learn a foreign language."

"Why?" asks the second. "That guy knew three, and it didn't do him any good!"

—ENGLISHFORUM.CH

I was buying airplane tickets when my 8-year-old asked, "Can a baby be considered a carry-on?" Before I could respond, my husband mumbled, "Well, it can definitely be considered baggage."

—BRIDGET SLAYDEN

As we drove into Traverse City, Michigan, we were greeted by a billboard advertising a restaurant in town. Its claim: "Steaks bigger than an 8th Street pothole."

—LOU ANN SWATZ

MAKE A BUCKET LIST; DO EVERYTHING ON THAT BUCKET LIST; MAKE ANOTHER BUCKET LIST.
—KATE HUDSON

Airplane travel is nature's way of making you look like your passport photo.
—AL GORE

I still enjoy traveling a lot. I mean, it amazes me that I still get excited in hotel rooms just to see what kind of shampoo they've left me.
—BILL BRYSON

Most of American life is driving somewhere and then driving back wondering why the hell you went.
—JOHN UPDIKE

Last year, complaints about airlines increased 22 percent. There were probably more complaints, but the airlines lost them.
—CONAN O'BRIEN

There ain't no surer way to find out whether you like people or hate them than to travel with them.
—MARK TWAIN

If God had really intended men to fly, he'd make it easier to get to the airport.
—GEORGE WINTERS

There are beach people, mountain people, lake people, and ocean people. I am a hotel person.
—JOHN KELLY

I haven't been everywhere, but it's on my list.
—SUSAN SONTAG

It can hardly be a coincidence that no language on earth has ever produced the expression "as pretty as an airport."
—DOUGLAS ADAMS

LAUGHTER IS AN INSTANT VACATION.
—MILTON BERLE

NUNS, SNAKES, AND BAD POLAROIDS

Travels with Dad were always a trip.

By **Melva Michaelian**

When I was 13, my parents decided to take my 9-year-old brother, Barry, and me on a trip to Canada. Before we left home, we stopped for a fill-up. The station owner—a friend of Dad's—suggested we stay at a place he knew just over the border. "It's run by some nuns," he added.

This was 1960, so navigation was done via giant folding map.

In Quebec, we bumped along back roads until we came to an edifice the size of a medieval abbey. Once inside, a nun brought us a big tureen of soup.

"Sister," my mother said, "it was our understanding that this is a hotel."

The nun shook her head. In broken English, she informed us that the place was, in fact, a homeless shelter. Horrified, Mom glared at Dad.

The nuns then arranged for us to stay with a farm family nearby. A boy showed Mom and me to a bed fitted with round jar caps filled with liquid.

"They are just to keep the snakes out," he reassured us. We clambered onto the bed, horrified, and didn't touch the floor the rest of the night.

The next morning, we heard Dad snapping Polaroids of our hosts. His pictures came out terrible, with vital body parts cut off.

The rest of our trip was just as eventful. In Quebec City, Dad tried to take our photo at the fortress above the St. Lawrence River, but he backed up too far and went over the wall.

In Montreal, he lost his wallet and we had to call my aunt to wire us money. Then Dad realized he'd lost our suitcases too.

More mishaps—including Dad and Barry sinking their rented paddleboat—didn't break our spirits. As we made our way home, Dad asked, "How about going to Washington next year?"

Unfortunately, we did.

3

TECH
TALK

When my son was visiting, I complained that my TV wasn't as bright and as sharp as it usually was. He worked on it during the afternoon, and that night, we turned the set on.

"What did you do?" I said happily. "Everything looks great now!"

He smugly replied, "I wiped the screen."

—BETTY BISHOP

I realized my little nephew will never know life without Facebook. He'll never know what it's like to go, "I wonder what happened to that guy Chris from high school?" and then just shrug his shoulders and move on.

—OPHIRA EISENBERG

When I find myself walking through the valley of the shadow of death, I remind myself not to trust Google Maps ever again.

—WILLIAM PETTICREW

Our new neighbors thought our Wi-Fi was our last name. So when they gave us a Christmas card, they addressed it to "The Linksys Family."

—HUFFINGTONPOST.COM

On the way to meet my husband at a restaurant, I realized that I didn't have my phone and immediately panicked. I needn't have worried. He'd seen my phone on the couch at home and brought it with him. When he arrived, I checked my texts. There was only one, and it was from him: "I'm on my way, and I have your phone."

—MICHELLE STEINMETZ

Accidentally closed a browser with 20+ tabs open. This must be what the scholars of Alexandria felt when their great library burned.

—@CAULIMOVIRUS

When I told my daughter's boyfriend that I didn't own a TV set, he was shocked.

"If you don't have a TV," he asked, "then how do you know how to arrange your furniture?"

—MEL VANNICE

My mother is still having trouble understanding just how her iPhone works. Upon receiving a text, she said to me, "Quick, give me a pencil so I can write this down."

—SANDRA NOVELLA

An Oregonian came home, heard rustling sounds from inside a bathroom, and could see a shadowy figure moving about underneath the closed door. The resident called police. They arrived, drew their guns, and ordered the prowler to come out with hands up. Receiving no response, they burst into the bathroom, where, according to a deputy, "We encountered a very thorough vacuuming job being done by a Roomba robotic vacuum cleaner."

—5NEWSONLINE.COM

I'm at the library, and when I plug my flash drive into the computer, it doesn't show up. I keep trying, but nothing happens. As an IT major, I know I can figure this out. So I spend 15 minutes changing settings and inserting and removing the flash drive. Then a girl sitting next to me taps my shoulder and says, "You're plugging it into my computer, not yours."

—ACIDCOW.COM

A large outdoor thermometer I had sent my son in Florida hung by his pool. One day he and his wife were standing beside it discussing the temperature. Scott was comparing the Fahrenheit scale to the Celsius scale when his 8-year-old daughter interrupted.

"Dad, is that what the F and the C on the thermometer mean?"

Told that was right, she said, "Gee, all this time I thought that they stood for Florida and Canada."

—JESSIE SNOW

Retail Therapy

■

Amazon thinks my recent humidifier purchase was merely the inaugural move in a newfound hobby of humidifier collecting.

—@JUSTINSHANES

Before you buy that nice jacket online, ask yourself, "Am I willing to delete one extra email every day for the rest of my life?"

—@AARONFULLERTON

It's a problem that the machine I use to do my work also has a function where you can shop for a new duvet cover for three hours.

—@CAITIEDELANEY

"I think we're named after computer passwords."

Five email addresses it would be annoying to give out loud:

- MikeUnderscore2004 @yahoo.com
- MikeAtYahooDot Com@hotmail.com
- Mike_WardAllOne Word@yahoo.com
- AAAAAAThatsSixAs @yahoo.com
- 1OneTheFirstJust TheNumberThe SecondSpelledOut @hotmail.com

—MICHAEL WARD, VIA MCSWEENEYS.NET

The computer in my high school classroom was acting up. After watching me struggle with it, a student explained that my hard drive had crashed. So I called IT.

"Can someone please look at my computer?" I asked. "The hard drive crashed."

"We can't just send people down on your say-so," said the specialist. "How do you know that's the problem?"

There are many theories on why humans even need to sleep, but I'm pretty sure it's to charge our phones.

—@ALISPAGNOLA

"A student told me."

"We'll send someone right over."

—THOMAS ELLSWORTH

Son to his father as they watch television: "Dad, tell me again how when you were a kid you had to walk all the way across the room to change the channel."

—BUCELLA IN VFW

Soon after texting a girl I liked, I received this response: "ERROR 3265 SWRVICE UNAVAILABLE." She never could spell.

—CHRISTOPHER THOMPSON

Trying to get online at my mother-in-law's, I scrolled through various internet access names. One neighbor's

Wi-Fi network really stood out: "You Kids Get Off My LAN!"

—NANCY LAWSON

My friend went to her doctor recently for a routine exam. First things first: getting weighed.

"We have a new digital scale with LED readout," boasted the nurse. My friend climbed on and was thrilled to see the screen read 127.

"Don't get too excited now," said the nurse. "That's the time."

—JANICE HYNE

Overheard: My 15-year-old niece fighting with her friend. "You think I can't live without you? Who do you think you are, my phone charger?"

—@ERUM_SANGJI

Scene: Me using the Siri app on my iPhone.

Me: Siri, call my wife.

Siri: Samantha McLaughlin is not in your contacts.

Me: Samantha Gibbs is my wife.

Siri: I've added Samantha Gibbs as your wife.

Me: Call my wife.

Siri: Which wife?

—TAYLOR GIBBS

My mother informed me one day that she had been using her smartphone to keep track of "all her important dates." She wasn't always the most tech-savvy person and was still figuring out the intricacies of her new gadget, so I was impressed that she had apparently been using the calendar app to stay organized. But then she turned her phone over to reveal the sticky note with a list of upcoming birthdays. As I started laughing, Mom asked bewilderedly, "What's wrong?"

—MATT DAVIS

As an assistant high school track coach, I recorded the results of each home meet and made copies for all the coaches. But because our track shed did not have electricity, I had to use carbon paper. A freshman team member offered to help, and I showed her how to place the carbon paper shiny side down so that the image would transfer to the sheet beneath it. "What will they think of next?" she said in astonishment. "Pretty soon we won't need copy machines anymore."

—BARBARA LOOMIS

I just read a great new novel on my Kindle. It was a real button-presser.

—PETER BACANIN

My email password has been hacked. That's the third time I've had to rename my cat.

—@D_JOYT

A few weeks ago, my dad decided he was going to order pizza from his iPad. He's almost finished.

—@SIMONCHOLLAND

A computer-illiterate client called the help desk asking how to change her password. "OK," I said, after punching in a few keys. "Log in using the password 123456." "Is that all in caps?" she asked.

—SUSAN KESSLER

"Have you tried turning it off and on again?"

Usually there's no computer problem I can't solve. But I met my match when I turned on my machine and was greeted with the message "Keyboard not detected. Hit any key to continue."

—ALEX HU

A real smart TV would increase the volume when you start eating chips.

—WERT52 ON REDDIT.COM

Soon after I started a new job, a coworker named Elizabeth showed me how to clear the copier when it became jammed. A few days later the machine jammed again, and I began to punch buttons and slam doors to clear it as I had been shown.

"What's going on?" asked a colleague.

"I'm clearing the copier like Elizabeth taught me," I replied.

"Oh, but you have to understand," the man explained. "Elizabeth has a temper."

—SHERRY MCNEAL

On the subway, untangling earbuds is the new knitting. The woman across from me could have finished a cardigan by now.

—GREG PREECE ON HUMORLABS.COM

needed a password eight characters long, so I picked Snow White and the Seven Dwarfs.

—NICK HELM

My grandfather raided his savings account to buy himself an advanced satellite TV system. After the installation, he had two huge satellite dishes in his backyard and a monstrous remote control in his hand.

Our entire family was there for the unveiling. Grandpa sat down in his easy chair and started flipping through hundreds of channels from all over the world. We went outside and saw the dishes rotating until they finally came to rest. When we went back into the living room to see what he had decided to watch, we found that he had gone to sleep in his chair.

—MICHAEL C. STONE

just found out my mum didn't know how to set the clock on her new microwave. So she stayed up until midnight and then plugged it in.

—@GIFTEDRASCAL

"I've got about 20 pages of questionable internet comments here."

The remote for our television broke, so my son went to get a new one at the electronics store. Later he called home.

"Mom, I forgot to bring it with me. What's the brand?"

I glanced at it and replied, "It's a Volch."

"A what?"

"V-o-l-c-h," I spelled.

"Mom," he sighed, "that's short for Volume and Channel."
—JOAN WHITE

Looking for the perfect Wi-Fi network name? Borrow one of these tried-and-true ones:

- I Pronounce You Man and Wi-Fi
- Wi-Fi Fo Fum
- Mom, Click Here for Internet
- Lord Voldemodem
- Click Here for Viruses
—RD.COM

Wit & Wordplay:
Abbreviation Elation
■

My wife and I had been texting back and forth when, unbeknownst to her, I had to stop for a few minutes. When I returned to my cellphone, I found this text message awaiting me: "CGYT?" "Huh?" I responded. She shot back: "Cat Got Your Thumb?"
—PAUL BROUN

Some texts should not be abbreviated. Case in point, this message from my cousin, which simply read "A J D." I was confused until my father called to tell me, "Aunt June died."
—MELODIE DIAZ CRUZ

"I'll miss you, Great-Grandma," my mother's great-grandson wrote in an email he sent before shipping out to Iraq. "I'll miss you too, dear," she responded. "Stay safe. LOL, Great-Grandma." Poor Mom didn't realize that LOL doesn't stand for "lots of love."
—JEANNE HENDRICKSON

My Roomba just went into the corner and knocked over the broom that was leaning there. Dude, chill out. You already got the job.
—@BURNIE

Pretty much the most frightening part of my day is when I get a notification that my mother has tagged me in a post on Facebook.
—@CULTUREDRUFFIAN

I've just reset my password to Delicate Luggage Handler, as I was told it had to be case-sensitive.
—@JULIANLEECOMEDY

PROWLING FOR DUST BUNNIES

Long before Marie Kondo, there was Roomba. In this classic from 2003, Mary Roach gives the robot vacuum cleaner a whirl.

By Mary Roach

I **have always** wanted for someone else to clean my house, as neither I nor my husband, Ed, has shown any aptitude for it. But I'd feel guilty inflicting such distasteful drudgery on another human. No one but me should have to clean up the dental floss heaped like spaghetti near the wastebasket.

Imagine my joy upon reading that the iRobot company has invented the Roomba. The website plays a clip of an enlarged CD Walkman scooting across a carpet, sucking up detritus. Meanwhile, sentences run across the screen: "I'm having lunch with a friend" ... "I'm planting flowers in the garden." The point is that you can "enjoy life" while your robot cleans up the conspicuous chunks strewn about your living room floor.

Roomba joined our family last week. Right away I changed the name to Reba, to indulge my fantasy of having a real cleaning person, yet still respecting its incredibly silly given name. As gadgets go, it's surprisingly simple to use. All you do is tell it the room size. This I calculated in my usual manner, by picturing six-foot guys lying end-to-end along the walls and multiplying accordingly.

I was on my way out the door to enjoy life when I heard a crash. Reba had tangled herself up in the telephone cord and then headed off in the other direction, pulling the phone off the nightstand. "Maybe she needs to make a call," said Ed.

I couldn't be annoyed, as I'm the sort of person who gets up to go to the bathroom on airplanes without unplugging my headphones. Only that my head is attached to my neck prevents it from being yanked off onto the floor. Also, it tells you right there in the owners manual to "pick up objects like clothing, loose papers … power cords … just as you would before using a regular vacuum."

This poses a problem in our house. The floor space along the walls and under the furniture in the office are filled with stacks of what I call Ed's desk runoff. My husband does not easily throw things away. Whatever he gets in the mail or empties from his pockets he simply deposits on the nearest horizontal surface.

Once a week, like a garbage truck, I throw Ed's discards onto the heaping landfill on his desk. At a certain point, determined by the angle of the slope and the savagery of my throws, the pile will begin to slide. This is Ed's cue to shovel it into a shopping bag, which he then puts on the floor with the intent to go through it later, later here meaning never.

Picking it all up for Reba would take more time than I normally spend vacuuming. It's the same situation that has kept me from hiring an assistant. It would take longer to explain my filing system ("Takeout menus and important contracts go in the orange folder labeled 'Bees' …") than it would to do the chore myself.

The bathroom promised to be less problematic. I put the hamper in the tub and the scale in the sink, where it looked as if it wanted a bath, or maybe had a date with a vacuum.

Then I went into the bedroom to fetch Reba, who was engaged in a shoving match with one of my Birkenstocks. She had pushed the shoe across the room and under the bed, well into the zone of no-reach.

"Good one," said Ed, who has always harbored ill will toward comfort footwear for women.

I aimed Reba at the grubby crawl space beneath the footed bathtub. I have tried this with Ed and various of my stepdaughters, but it always fails to produce the desired effect.

Reba was not only willing but enthusiastic about the prospect, motoring full bore under the tub and whacking her forehead on the far wall. You just can't find help like that.

The living room was a similar success. Reba does housework much like I do, busily cleaning in one spot and then wandering off inexplicably and getting distracted by something else. iRobot calls this an "algorithm-based cleaning pattern," a term I will use the next time Ed catches me polishing silver while the mop water evaporates in the other room.

Halfway across the carpet, Reba emitted undelighted noises. Ed leafed through the troubleshooting guide.

"It's a Whimper Beep," he said in the concerned baritone that once announced the Heartbreak of Psoriasis as if it were the Cuban Missile Crisis. Wound around Reba's brushes was a two-foot strand of dental floss. Apparently even robots have their limits.

Not everyone has mastered the art of texting. Case in point:

Mom: Stop at dollar store on way home and get lunch maggots.

Me: Lunch maggots?

Mom: Baffles.

Mom: Baggies.

Mom: Ziploc lunch Baggies.

Mom: Spell-check is not helping me.

Mom: By the way, this is Dad.

—WHENPARENTSTEXT .COM

Computers are great for modernizing the world, putting information at our fingertips, and keeping techies busy answering very silly customer questions like this:

Tech Support: Click on the My Computer icon to the left of the screen.

Customer: Are you talking about your left or mine?

—ANNA HANSEN

When my printer's type began to grow faint, I called a local repair shop, where a friendly man informed me that the printer probably needed only to be cleaned. Because the store charged $50 for such cleanings, he told me, I might be better off reading the printer's manual and trying the job myself. Pleasantly surprised by his candor, I asked, "Does your boss know that you discourage business?"

"Actually it's my boss's idea," the employee replied sheepishly. "We usually make more money on repairs if we let people try to fix things themselves first."

—MICHELLE R. ST. JAMES

Everyone hates millennials until it's time to convert a PDF into a Word document.

—@SARAMVALENTINE

Outraged by the high fees her computer consultants charged, a friend asked my dad which service he used.

"My sons," he said. "They both earned degrees in computer science."

"So you get the work done for nothing," the friend marveled.

Dad smiled and said, "Actually, I figured it cost me about $40,000 for my kids to fix my computer for free."

—RYAN GILLESPIE

When I was a kid, my parents taught me to not believe everything I saw on TV. Now I have to teach them to not believe everything they see on Facebook.

—SNICKSOUND ON REDDIT.COM

"It keeps me from looking at my phone every two seconds."

My 5-year-old son was begging us to get him an iPad.

"My friend brought his to school last week, and I want one too," he insisted.

"Absolutely not," said my husband. "They're fragile and much too expensive. Besides, what would you even do with an iPad?"

Our son replied, "I'd put it over my eye and play pirates with my friends."

—JULIE R.

I asked my friend about the pros and cons of using a Kindle as opposed to just getting the Kindle app.

"Oh, the Kindle is way better," she said. "Because it's an actual book."

—JANET WOHLGEMUT

I finally convinced my mother that she should learn to text. Her first message to me: "Whereisthespacebar?"

—CINDY RODEN

I'll call it a "smart" phone the day I yell "Where's my phone?" and it yells "Down here! In the couch cushions!"

—@HERE_TO_LAUGH

Tech Support: What does the screen say now?
Customer: It says, "Hit Enter when ready."
Tech Support: Well?
Customer: How do I know when it's ready?

—BECQUET.COM

"Would you please stop reading over my shoulder?"

I've started wearing a fitness tracker to count my daily steps, and the first time I made it to 9,989 steps in one day, I proudly showed the device to my stepson.

"Not bad," he said. "But you'd better keep walking. You're looking at it upside down."

—JENNY JOHNSON

Adam and Eve: the first people not to read the Apple Terms and Conditions.

—CHURCH SIGN,
VIA PLANET PROCTOR
NEWSLETTER

My computer just gave me an "Error 404" message, which can't be right, because I know I've made way more errors than that.

—@DMC1138

I used my new navigation app to help me find my way to a writers' conference. After a long drive, I parked my car and, first things first, immediately headed for the crowded restroom. I found a stall and settled in. That's when a loud, clear voice from my phone announced, "You've arrived at your destination!"

—ANITA MORRISON

Just walked up a flight of stairs, and my Fitbit emailed me to report itself stolen.

—@THECATWHISPERER

Scene: A local bar.
Me: What's the Wi-Fi password?
Bartender: You need to buy a drink first.
Me: OK, I'll have a Coke.
Bartender: That'll be three dollars.

Scientists now say that people should not use their cellphones outdoors during thunderstorms because of the risk of being struck by lightning. You should also avoid using them in movie theaters because of the risk of being strangled.

—BEN WALSH

Me: There you go. So what's the password?
Bartender: "You need to buy a drink first." No spaces, all lowercase.

—SYLVIA MCCLAIN

I just set my email's auto-response to "I'm looking into this now. I'll let you know." I will literally never have to respond to emails again.

—@9TO5LIFE

I hate it when I forget my password and can't answer my secret questions right. It's like I don't even know me.

—@KWIRKYKERRI

My mother's maiden name is Password.

—@TYLERLINKIN

I DON'T BELIEVE IN EMAIL. I'M AN OLD-FASHIONED GIRL. I PREFER CALLING AND HANGING UP.

—SARAH JESSICA PARKER

I didn't realize how good I was with computers until I met my parents.

—MIKE BIRBIGLIA

Watching a teenager on his smartphone, I realized that the idiom "all thumbs" might be doomed.

—CALVIN TRILLIN

If I'm ever feeling down, I just type "Yo are the best" into Google. Then it responds, "I think you mean: You are the best." And I feel much better.

—JACK BERRY

I took a 2-year-old computer in to be repaired, and the guy looked at me as though he was a gun dealer and I'd brought him a musket. In two years, I'd gone from cutting-edge to Amish.

—JON STEWART

I had to take my son's phone from him, which is the worst thing to do to a child. He broke down. He said, "Take my leg instead."

—KEVIN HART

Every time I almost think humanity will be OK, I see someone struggle with the self-checkout for 20 minutes.

—CAPRICE CRANE

Before you marry a person, you should first make them use a computer with slow internet to see who they really are.

—WILL FERRELL

A COMPUTER ONCE BEAT ME AT CHESS, BUT IT WAS NO MATCH FOR ME AT KICK BOXING.

—EMO PHILIPS

MESSAGE RECEIVED, LOUD AND CLEAR

A misplaced cellphone could have caused quite a buzz.

By Anita Stafford

Life was much simpler when telephones were fixed objects.

These days, I lose my cellphone at least once a day. I usually find it somewhere I've absentmindedly left it, but recently I had an episode that caused me to stop being so careless.

It was a Sunday morning, and I was preparing to go to church. After dressing and tidying up the bathroom, I could not find my cellphone. I retraced my steps but had no luck. Without a landline, I didn't have the option of calling my missing phone. And my husband was traveling, so I didn't have his phone to help locate mine. Not wanting to be late, I gave up the search and left.

I arrived at church, squeezing past a bunch of people so I could sit beside my mother. I was lucky she'd saved me a seat—the pews were full.

After the service, I shook my neighbors' hands and visited with good friends before driving home. Pulling into the garage, I was startled to hear a phone ring.

I looked around, puzzled. The phone rang again, and this time I felt a concurrent vibration inside my shirt. Then came an epiphany: I had slipped the cellphone inside my bra that morning because my outfit had no pockets. Then I had worn the phone to church with the ringer volume set at full blast.

I went pale at the thought of what would have happened if the cellphone had gone off at church.

Would I have let it ring, ignoring the noise coming from inside my blouse? Would I have reached into my unmentionables to retrieve the thing while those around me gasped? Would I have simply died on the spot while blushing profusely?

After teetering on the verge of such a faux pas, I needed to share my confession. You could say I felt compelled to "get it off my chest."

TEN-DOLLAR
WORDS

The homework assignment for my Spanish class was to write a paragraph. When I returned their papers, I asked one student if he had used Google Translate or any other online translator to write his paper. He categorically denied doing so. That led to my next question: "Then why is this in French?"

—MARY-TERESA PLATT

My son, stationed in Japan, dated a Japanese girl who spoke little English. That didn't faze him until the night she announced, "I have chicken pox." My son didn't know whether to run or get her to the hospital. Then he noticed her shiver.

"You don't have chicken pox," he said, relieved. "You have goose bumps."

—NEJLA WILLIAMS BODINE

A linguistics professor is lecturing his class.

"In English," he says, "a double negative forms a positive. However, in Russian, a double negative remains a negative. But there isn't a single language, not one, in which a double positive can express a negative."

Suddenly, a voice from the back shouts out: "Yeah, right."

—VIRALNOVA.COM

Words you'd think were really cool if you didn't know what they mean:
- atrophy
- space bar
- supervision
- extraction
- dogmatic

—@DANMENTOS

The other day, my granddaughter's husband was griping about how spell-check changes the meaning of emails when his friend, an Air Force officer, told him this story: He'd sent a message to 300 of his personnel addressed to "Dear Sirs and Ma'ams." It was received as "Dear Sirs and Mamas."

—PHYLLIS HOWARD

Our booking office had three phones. One day during lunch, I was responsible for answering all of them. It was a constant repeat of "May I help you?" or "Will you hold?" I guess I got confused, because I surprised one man on the other end of the line when I answered his call with "May I hold you?"

—VERA GRANGER

Anagrams **of** "Ernest Hemingway" that could also be titles of Hemingway novels:

- Seething Wary Men
- When Gin May Steer
- The Enemy War Sign
- We Earthy Men Sing
- Anywhere Gins Met
- Yes, New Nightmare

—SARAH ASWELL ON MCSWEENEYS.NET AND READER'S DIGEST STAFF

My grandson came home from kindergarten in tears.

"What's wrong?" his mother asked.

"The teacher told us to eat the popcorn and then we could read," he said.

"So?"

Now sobbing, he said, "I ate all the popcorn, and I still can't read!"

—BARBARA MURPHY

I enjoy collecting malapropisms. Here are some good ones: "Sitting back on one's hinges." "Bull in a china closet." "Nip it in the butt." My favorite came in response to a first aid questionnaire handed out by my women's group. To the question "If someone was choking, what would you do?" one person wrote, "I would perform the Hamlet Maneuver."

—VIRGINIA COOK

My job as a facilities maintenance engineer required a wide range of skills. One day I might have to fix the furnace, while the next day could see me painting the CEO's office. When I described it to a coworker as "I'm a jack of all trades, master of none," I was amused, yet slightly offended, when she offered a less than complimentary

Q: What's the difference between a cat and a comma?

A: One has claws at the end of its paws, and the other is a pause at the end of a clause.

—RD.COM

interpretation from her native Cantonese: "Equipped with knives all over, yet none are very sharp."

—CHARLES GOETZINGER

Mineralogy? The study of minerals. Oceanology? The study of oceans. Meteorology? NOT ABOUT METEORS.

—@ADAMOFEARTH

I was bemoaning to a friend how my last name, Loyer, is frequently changed to "Lawyer" by spell-check.

"I can top that," he said. He's an anesthesiologist named Bause. "But," he said, "spell-check insists on calling me Dr. Abuse."

—MILTON LOYER

Every Christmas season, my 4-year-old granddaughter, Jordan, helps me set up my nativity scene. It has many small pieces: the stable, the manger, baby Jesus, animals, shepherds, an angel, and the three wise men. This year, she wanted to do it all by herself. After much arranging and rearranging of things, she started to cry.

"Jordan," I said, "what's the matter?"

She replied, "Grandma, I don't know where to put the wise guys."

—J.D.

I texted my husband to tell him that I'd be out of touch for a bit since I planned to color my hair. Thanks to autocorrect, here's what he read: "After I finish my cup of coffee, I am going to die. You may not be able to reach me while I'm in the midst of that."

—KRISTINE BINACO

An Englishman, a Frenchman, a Spaniard, and a German are watching a street performer. The performer suddenly realizes that these men have a poor view, so he gets on a small platform. "Can you all see me now?" he asks them. They respond: "Yes." "Oui." "Sí." "Ja."

—JUSTSOMETHING.CO

5 Hilarious Literal Translations

■

SARATAN EL BAHR (ARABIC)
Translation: "cancer of the sea"
What we call it: lobster

JOULUPUKKI (FINNISH)
Translation: "Christmas billy goat"
What we call it: Santa Claus

DIÀNNǍO (MANDARIN)
Translation: "electric brain"
What we call it: computer

STOFZUIGER (DUTCH)
Translation: "dust sucker"
What we call it: vacuum

NACKTSCHNECKE (GERMAN)
Translation: "naked snail"
What we call it: slug

—MENTALFLOSS.COM

PUTTING MY WORD-OF-THE-DAY CALENDAR TO GOOD USE

Get just a little too wordy, and you'll have everyone around you irked, miffed, and exasperated.

By Jeremy Woodcock

JANUARY 1

A new year ahead, full of *auspicious* and promising things! Think I'll stop by Dairy Queen for a Blizzard, but is that too *auspicious* this early in the year? Hard to say. Hard to say.

JANUARY 2

Had a fun breakfast with my girlfriend, Meredith. *Risible*, even. Later, I had a *risible* chat with Jeff at the watercooler.

It's nice to be back at work, though my holidays were pretty *risible*, too, by which I guess I mean a situation or thing having qualities by which to provoke laughter and/or amusement.

JANUARY 3

Packed some pasta *puttanesca* for lunch today. I had a big presentation to make, which went downhill quickly when I described our first-quarter profits as having "the consistency of a *pasta puttanesca*," and my boss kept asking me to clarify what I meant. I tried, but he just got angrier, turning red like *you know what*.

JANUARY 4

Today's page was missing from my calendar! How *vexing*! Meredith had said that might happen, since the box seemed to have been opened when I bought it. I didn't find it *vexing* at the time, but I guess I should have because now it's very *vexing* to have had this happen! In the end, I just skipped to tomorrow's word.

JANUARY 5

Another *vexing* day.

JANUARY 6

Meredith asked whether I'd go to the new Jennifer Lawrence movie with her. I said sure, but she'd have to check the times, since I'm not a *soothsayer*. Suddenly she asked me to sit down. She said I'd been acting weird and insisted that things had to change. OK, so just tell me that next time! I can't guess—I'm not a *soothsayer*.

JANUARY 7
Today's events can be summed up in one word: *esplanade*.

JANUARY 8
Meredith broke up with me. I can't really *glean* why. I said, "Meredith, can you please move your stuff off the kitchen table? I can barely see the newspaper I'm reading to *glean* what happened in the world today!" Next thing I could *glean*, she'd lost it.

JANUARY 9
Got fired today. It happened in a really *pusillanimous* way. I'm just working at my desk when my boss suddenly comes over and starts asking me whether I've been feeling OK. I mentioned my recent breakup but insisted it would be pretty *pusillanimous* to let that get me down. Next thing I knew, all my possessions, including my calendar, were in a box, and I was headed out the door.

JANUARY 10
I'm still hopeful, despite recent *dyspeptic* events. I'm using my extra time to hasten my *pilgrimage* through my calendar. Now I can take a minute, an hour, or even a *yoctosecond* to really *ruminate* over that thing. I've been a bit *itinerant* lately, but I can *vouchsafe* that things will *ameliorate* from here.

JANUARY 11
Lost my word-of-the-day calendar. Oh boy. This is *vexing*.

"I'm going to forgo all the gobbledygook and cut straight to the rigamarole."

I was at the hardware store to get a duplicate of my car key made when the store clerk asked, "You're a model?" It was exactly what a woman in her mid-30s wanted to hear. "Well, no, I'm not," I said, blushing. "But I'm very flattered that—" He stopped me right there, pointed to my car keys, and repeated slowly, "Year ... and ... model?"

—KIIRSTEN JEPPSON

My boyfriend worked in a posh hotel, and at breakfast someone asked, "Is this crème fraîche?" He replied, "Yeah, we don't serve out-of-date food here."

—@LILYANNATRNR

My wife and I were having lunch at a fashionable eatery in Annapolis when we noticed what looked like a familiar face at the next table. Screwing up my courage, I asked, "Excuse me. Aren't you Marlin Fitzwater, the former White House press secretary?"

"Yes, I am," he acknowledged, and graciously interrupted his lunch to talk to us. As we were leaving the restaurant, I remarked to the hostess, "Do you know you have Marlin Fitzwater out on the terrace?"

"I'm not sure about that," she replied, "but we have Perrier and Evian at the bar."

—BRUCE F. HENDERSON

Every year I spell Hanukkah differently, and it's correct every time.

—@HOBO_SPLENDIDO

Most of my English literature classmates thought reading Melville's *Billy Budd* would be an easy task because the novel is only 90 pages long. One boy, however, complained that the text was heavy and hard to comprehend.

"Hey," another student suggested, "maybe you should try reading Budd Light."

—CARRIE L. BENSON

Yes, I may have misheard you, but this doesn't mean I don't want a night cat any less.

—@ROYAL_STEIN

People found guilty of not using punctuation deserve the longest sentence possible.

—@SIXTHFORMPOET

In many cultures, people believe that you can protect a baby from evil spirits by not complimenting him or her, lest the fates get jealous. So in Thailand, you might hear an adult coo something like "Fatty" or "Pig." In Bulgaria, adults pretend to spit and insult the baby by saying things like "May the chickens poop on you."

—JOYCE EISENBERG AND ELLEN SCOLNIC, IN *STUFF EVERY GRANDMOTHER SHOULD KNOW*

Harry Potter is on and my dad thinks Voldemort's name is Baltimore.

—@DUBSTEP4DADS

My sister tried on my brother's new eyeglasses and asked how she looked.

"Very astute," I replied. Annoyed, she shot back, "I think I look intelligent!"

—SUSAN SHAFER

Autocorrect can go straight to he'll.

—CONSTANCE NORMANDEAU

My friend had been pounding the pavement in search of a job with no luck. Frustrated, she asked her dad to look at her résumé. He didn't get much further than the first line of her cover letter before spotting the problem.

"Is it too generic?" she asked.

"I doubt it," said her father. "Especially since it's addressed 'Dear Sir or Madman.'"

—GISELLE MELANSON

Wit & Wordplay:
Pronunciation Woes
∎

Thinking about the time that I said that I was distantly related to Marie Curie and a guy explained, "It's pronounced Mariah Carey."

—@I_LEAN

During my time in the Navy, everyone was getting KP or guard duty except me. Not wanting to get in trouble, I asked the ensign why. "What's your name?" he asked. "Michael Zyvoloski." "That's why. I can't pronounce it, much less spell it."

—MICHAEL J. ZYVOLOSKI

My friend struck up a conversation with a stranger. When the stranger asked where she was from, my friend replied, "Iowa." "Where?" "Iowa. I-owe-uh." "Oh," said the woman. "Where I'm from, we pronounce it 'Oh-hi-oh.'"

—H. ELAINE PARSONS

"Sorry I'm late. Two roads diverged in a wood, and I took the one less traveled by..."

Is it coincidence that you can rearrange the letters in the first phrase in each pair to get the phrase after the equal sign?

- Dormitory = Dirty room
- The Morse code = Here come dots
- Slot machines = Cash lost in 'em
- Snooze alarms = Alas! No more z's
- Eleven plus two = Twelve plus one

—AHAJOKES.COM

It's such poor planning that *ninja* doesn't have at least one silent letter.

—@UNFITZ

If lawyers can be disbarred and clergymen can be defrocked, doesn't it follow that electricians can be delighted, musicians denoted, and cowboys deranged?

—VIRGINIA OSTMAN

A thesaurus is great. There's no other word for it.

—ROSS SMITH

My 11-year-old takes his homework seriously. One question required him to write a sentence using the word *version*. His sentence: "Have you heard of the version Mary?"

—RON WILLIAMS JR.

I learned from an early age that my name is spelled oddly, so I make a point of bringing it up to others if they need to spell it. When I bought my first set of furniture, the salesperson asked for my name to put on the contract. I said it was Philip, one l. He then asked me for my home address.

"Don't you want my last name?" I asked. He looked confused and said that I had already given it to him. I looked at the contract, and sure enough, there it 'was: "Phillip Wannel."

—PHILIP NICKISCH

At a loss for words? So were these befuddled employees:
■ I couldn't remember the term *lab coat*, so I had to go with "science blazer."

—@RUSTMONSTER

■ I am a librarian, and I forgot the word *book*. So I told a new patron, "We have a diverse selection of thingies."

—@DUNSLIBRARIAN

■ I forgot the word *articulate* in an interview and instead said, "I'm good at saying things."

—@KATHY_HIRST

Never leave alphabet soup on the stove and then leave the house. It could spell disaster.

—RD.COM

On her first day of rounds at an Australian hospital, a visiting American nurse meets an old man packing up.

"I'm going home to die," he says.

Alarmed, she quickly checks his chart.

"Not according to this, you aren't."

"I'm going home to die!" he insists.

"Who told you that?"

"My doctor."

"Well, it's not true. You are not going home to die!"

"Yes, I am! I was supposed to go home yester-die, but instead, I'm going home to-die!"

—DOROTHY SMITH

We adopted our daughter from China when she was 9, and we soon discovered that common American phrases and idioms didn't come easily. Case in point, the time she tried to praise me for being outgoing and having lots of friends. With a great big smile she declared, "When I grow up, I want to be a big mouth just like you!"

—AMY REYNOLDS

"So, the memo said '21-gnu salute,' huh?"

PAGING DR. MALAPROP!

Mixing medical jargon with voice recognition software
can cause a real headache.

By MK Wolfe

My work as a medical transcriptionist (MT) brings me in intimate contact with voice recognition (VR) software. We MTs listen to a doctor's dictation while reviewing the VR's first pass at the typewritten medical record and edit as we go.

Now, I know voice recognition is technically just a series of digital ones and zeros in a particular order, but I have come to believe that the software has a mind of its own—that there's a ghost in the machine, if you will. VR software can decipher thick accents talking at lightning speed using dense medical terminology and get it right. But it is also comically stupid, as these real examples reveal.

Take names. Does *McRoberts* really sound like *Crab Birds*? What kind of software listens to ordinary names and hears *Mr. Breakfast, Ms. Pulseless, Dr. Mean Itch, Ms. The Kittens, Dr. Ominous*, and *Mr. Loop Brains*?

In one single physical, a Mr. Morton was identified variously as *Mr. Morton* (good job, VR!), *Mr. Martin, Mr. Marvin, Mr. More, Mr. Morgan, Mr. Mortise*, and *Mr. Morabito*.

Really? No problem spelling *mediastinal lymphadenopathy* in that report, though.

As to the personality of the VR, it's most like that of a teenage male, obsessed with scatological humor. As if it were scrawling on a bathroom stall, the machine turns *3.5 mm Resolute stent* into *3.5 mm rather lewd stent*. I can just hear it giggling as it turns *Oh, I'm sorry* into *orange diarrhea*. I can see it wrinkling its virtual nose in disgust, turning *gynecologic* ("Ewww, girlie stuff!") into *title thought clot sick*.

Food is another favorite topic. *Minnesota* is, of course, *then a soda*, while *sarcopenia*, which is age-related muscle loss, turns into *sauerkraut anemia*. (I can't imagine how the machine learned about sauerkraut.) The poor soul with Takotsubo syndrome, a temporarily weakened heart muscle, is thought to instead have *taco bowl syndrome*—clearly, that patient must also be a teenager. But when someone who is essentially hemiparetic (weakened on one side) is instead thought by the machine to be a *chili pepper radical*, we wonder just how educated this machine really is. It must have had a rough time in college—the University of Missouri is disdainfully referred to by the VR as *the University of Misery*.

As with many teenagers, girls are constantly on the VR's mind. Doctor: "We will continue to monitor her, but ..." VR (leeringly): "We will continue to monitor her buttocks ..." When a doctor dictates "We are going to try to get her heart pumping better," the machine gleefully announces "We are going to try to get her heart clubbing better." This makes some degree of sense, because though the doctor opines "She appears acute," the machine proclaims "She appears cute."

The VR does show occasional glimmers of intelligence—even rowdy teens learn some wisdom sometimes. One contrite VR, when listing consultations made on a patient, heard "Number one, Interventional Radiology," but chose to add, completely unsolicited, a number two—"Mother." Yes, one should always consult one's mother, don't you think?

And so, "this ends dictation," or as the VR interprets that, "descending stairs."

Many years ago, my two sons spent time coaching their toddler sister to say something special to me on Mother's Day. They had been teaching her "You are priceless." Certain that she had the words lined up right, they watched, peeking out from behind their door, as their little sister made her way down the hall. She called out to me and then proudly announced, "Mommy, you are worthless."

—HELEN L. ZIMMERMAN

As a kindergarten teacher, I work with students of many different reading abilities. One day, I was helping a student who was struggling to learn the letter sounds. I used flash cards with letters and pictures to help. I showed him the letter *s* and a picture of a snake to emphasize the sound. *Sss*, snake. Next came the letter *c*. He couldn't remember the sound, so I showed him a picture of a cat. When I asked him to tell me the sound of *c*, he looked puzzled and said, "Meow?"

—AIMEE ASHBY

During a conference, my high school principal insulted my immigrant mother's English. Mom didn't get upset. Instead, she smiled politely as she delivered this punch to the gut: "I'm sorry. Sometimes I get English mixed up with the six other languages I speak."

—REDDIT.COM

Shortly after my son started college, the president of the university had an assembly for the new students. "Welcome to Johns Hopkins," he began, "and please note that it's Johns, not John."

Then he told of how one of his predecessors, Milton Eisenhower, had been invited to talk at the University of Pittsburgh. After he was introduced as the president of "John Hopkins," Eisenhower said, "Thank you. It's great to be in Pittsburgh."

—JOSEPH B. MIRSKY

"What does the word *contemplate* mean?" a college student asked his English professor.

"Think about it," the professor answered.

"Ugh!" the student groaned. "Can't you just tell me?"

—DANA THAYER

I'm not saying that my daughter is overly dramatic. I'm just reminding you that she calls tears "wet drops of sad."

—@LETMESTART

"It's a common error. I'm a bison, but I'm from Buffalo."

We've all heard jokes that start with "A man walks into a bar ..." Here's what might happen if an English major had a say in the matter:

- Two quotation marks walk into a "bar."
- Hyperbole totally rips into this insane bar and absolutely destroys everything.
- A non sequitur walks into a bar. In a strong wind, even turkeys can fly.
- A mixed metaphor walks into a bar, seeing the handwriting on the wall but hoping to nip it in the bud.
- A cliché walks into a bar—fresh as a daisy, cute as a button, and sharp as a tack.
- A malapropism walks into a bar, looking for all intensive purposes like a wolf in cheap clothing, muttering epitaphs.
- A synonym strolls into a tavern.

—BLUEBIRDOF BITTERNESS.COM

While out walking with my son, a doctor, I fell and cut my hand. Quickly realizing that the injury would require sutures, he voice-texted his nurse: "My mom has a bad cut. I'm on the way to the office to sew her up." His "smart" phone transcribed the last part of his message: "I am on the way to the office to sober up."

—TERRY KELLEN

I'm known as a stickler for good spelling. So when an associate emailed technical documents and asked me to "decifer" them, I had to set him straight.

"*Decipher* is spelled with a *ph*, not an *f*," I wrote. "In case you've forgotten, spell-checker comes free with your Microsoft program."

A minute later came his reply: "Mine must be dephective."

—NORMAN MIDDLETON

Our family was playing the game Outburst. One of the topics was the Ten Commandments. Everyone shouted over one another as we called out answers, including my 8-year-old grandson, who yelled, "Thou shalt not admit adultery!"

—BARBARA STEVENS

My laptop was driving me crazy. "The A, E, and I keys always stick," I complained to a friend. She quickly diagnosed the problem. "Your computer is suffering from irritable vowel syndrome."

—ANGIE BULAKITES

A **man is** at the funeral of an old friend. He tentatively approaches the deceased's wife and asks whether he can say a word. The widow nods. The man clears his throat and says, "Plethora." The widow smiles appreciatively.

"Thanks," she says. "That means a lot."

—ROB KIENER

and set it on the scale. It weighed precisely 8 ounces. Impressed, I asked, "How did you know?" Looking pleased with himself, he declared, "I'm psychotic."

—GLADYS HOCUTT

D **uring a** game of Scrabble, my aunt decided to pass.

"I simply can't move my vowels," she complained. My uncle replied, "Why? Are you consonated?"

—SUZANNE CARLSON

W **hat should** you say to comfort a ruffled grammar fanatic? Easy—"There, their, they're."

—RD.COM

O **ur assistant** principal called in one of my underperforming Intro to Spanish pupils to ask why he was having trouble with the subject.

"I don't know. I just don't understand Ms. Behr," the boy said. "It's like she's speaking another language."

—MARCIA BEHR

A **fter I asked** for a half-pound trout fillet at my supermarket's seafood counter, the clerk picked one out of a pile

Testing, Testing

■

The note I left on my student's middle school test said: "Please look up the meanings of *suppository* and *depository*." It was in response to a question he'd answered concerning where Lee Harvey Oswald was when he assassinated President Kennedy.

—KAREN SKOPHAMMER

My daughter was typing up a test for a religion class she teaches. The answer to one question was "Joseph of Arimathea." The computer obviously disagreed and, thanks to spell-check, changed it to "Joseph of Aroma Therapy."

—RUTH ANN CAMPBELL

PEOPLE WILL ACCEPT YOUR IDEAS MUCH MORE READILY IF YOU TELL THEM BENJAMIN FRANKLIN SAID IT FIRST.

—DAVID H. COMINS

A synonym is a word you use when you can't spell the first word you thought of.

—BURT BACHARACH

Why is it a penny for your thoughts but you have to put your two cents in? Somebody's making a penny.

—STEVEN WRIGHT

We can teach kids there's no I in team, but it's way more important to teach them that there's no a in definitely.

—AARON FULLERTON

Delete the adjectives and [you'll] have the facts.

—HARPER LEE

Always and never are two words you should always remember never to use.

—WENDELL JOHNSON

A joke is truth concentrate—the most amount of truth in the shortest amount of words.

—LARRY WILMORE

Always read stuff that will make you look good if you die in the middle of it.

—P.J. O'ROURKE

It's a strange world of language in which skating on thin ice can get you into hot water.

—FRANKLIN P. JONES

MY FATHER ALWAYS SAID, "NEVER TRUST ANYONE WHOSE TV IS BIGGER THAN THEIR BOOKSHELF."

—EMILIA CLARKE

SHAKESPEARE LOVER "NOT-TO-BE"

Sophomoric humor couldn't help one student make the grade.

By Ed Withrow

*L*eaning against her desk in front of our class, Miss Hoover eagerly read aloud the words of William Shakespeare.

A few students actually seemed to like the Bard, but most more or less tolerated him, because they knew their semester grade would depend upon it. For me, even tolerance was too much to ask. I chose to ignore the ongoing dramatic reading entirely. Instead, I spent my classroom time ogling pretty girls and trying, mostly unsuccessfully, to throw paper clips into the heating vent. In between such activities, I dozed off a few times.

Suddenly, I snapped awake as Miss Hoover closed her book and placed it on her desk with a decisive thud.

Then she made an unexpected announcement. "Lovely, lovely, lovely!" she trilled. "I'm certain that all of you, even Edward Withrow"—that part was said with a malicious smirk—"have enjoyed these words."

"Now each of you will write an essay of 2,000 words detailing your personal thoughts on *As You Like It*. Please have your assignments on my desk on Monday morning."

Monday morning arrived. Everyone turned in his or her assignment, and all but mine were several pages thick. My single page looked like this:

Edward Withrow
Sophomore Class
English Literature

As You Like It
by William Shakespeare

I didn't. (Ditto it 1,000 times.)

Need I even say that Miss Hoover failed to appreciate the humor?

LOVE &
MARRIAGE

Jeff's blind date with Suzanne was bad from the start—in short, they loathed each other. Fortunately, Jeff had asked his friend to call him so he'd have an excuse to leave if the date wasn't going well. When his friend called, Jeff pretended to be in shock.

"I have to leave," Jeff said to Suzanne. "My aunt just died."

"Thank goodness," Suzanne replied. "If yours hadn't, mine would've had to."

—FROM LAUGH OFF
BY BOB FENSTER

While I was volunteering in a local soup kitchen, I hit it off with a very attractive single man. It was a relief, since it had become a running joke in my family that the men to whom I was drawn were inevitably married. So, feeling optimistic about my chances, I asked my new friend what he did for a living. He replied, "I'm a priest."

—LISA SHASHA

Prior to dinner, my 80-year-old mother-in-law stopped off at the beauty parlor.

"All the women did was complain about their husbands," she said over our entrees.

"Did you complain about your husband?" I asked, adding a sly nod toward my father-in-law.

"I didn't have to," she said. "They all know him."

—CYNTHIA BOEHNING

As I stripped off my sweatshirt at the breakfast table one morning, the T-shirt I was wearing underneath it started to come off too.

My husband let out a low whistle. I took it as a compliment until he said, from behind his newspaper, "Can you believe the price of bananas?"

—BEATRICE ROCHE

When people hear that my husband and I just celebrated our 60th wedding anniversary, they inevitably ask us the secret to our long, successful marriage. In response, my husband will smile sweetly, nod my way, and explain, "We both love me."

—MARIAN PITCHER

"Dear, if you'll make the toast and pour the juice,"
said the newlywed bride, "breakfast will be ready."
"Good! What are we having for breakfast?" her hubby asked.
"Toast and juice," said the bride.

—THEADVOCATE.COM

My then-wife and I were going through a divorce when we sat together to watch a TV show. It was about a New York City transit cop, played by James Brolin, who was rescuing passengers trapped in a flooded subway. To my pleasant surprise, my wife said, "He's only an actor. You're trained to do that. Scout, Army, NYPD Rescue ... You could really save them, not him." It was a sweet moment that ended when she remarked, "Of course, he looks much better doing it."

—ALBERT WEIR

One morning, Emma woke up with a start. Her husband, Jim, asked what the matter was.

"I had a dream that you gave me a pearl necklace for Valentine's Day," she said. "What could it mean?"

"You'll find out tonight," Jim said slyly. That evening, Jim came home with a small package for his wife. Emma ripped open the wrapping paper, tore into the box, and pulled out her gift— a book titled *The Meaning of Dreams*.

—THETRENDINSIGHTS .COM

My husband and I get along better since realizing how much our yelling upsets the dog.

—@DARLAINKY

A woman rubbed a lamp and out popped a genie.

"Do I get three wishes?" she asked.

"Nope, I'm a one-wish genie. What will it be?"

"See this map? I want these countries to stop fighting so we can have world peace."

"They've been at war for thousands of years. I'm not that good," he said. "What else do you have?"

"Well, I'd love a good man. One who's considerate, loves kids, likes to cook, and doesn't watch sports all day."

"OK," the genie said with a sigh. "Let me see that map again."

—D. RICHARDS

Recently I woke up in a particularly good mood. So much so that I felt compelled to look over at my husband and say, "Honey, I love you." He returned my gaze and asked, "Why? What's the matter?"

—KATHLEEN SMITH

Confronting my husband, I demanded, "How come you never tell me I look pretty? Even my sisters tell me I look pretty sometimes." "Your sisters are absolutely right," he said grandly. "You do look pretty sometimes."

—ALICE FAY

"I'm looking for a card that says 'Your Love Is Priceless' for under $5."

Movies show people kissing in the rain, but I want a guy who'll run out there and get the cushions off the porch chairs when the weather starts kicking up.

—@ANNIEMUMARY

Although I'd been dating a woman for several months, I guess I didn't know her as well as I thought. One day I called, and her 10-year-old son answered the phone.

"Hi there," I said. "It's Tom. Can I speak with your mom?"

"Sure," he responded. "Are you Tom One or Tom Two?"

Needless to say, his mother is now down to one Tom.

—THOMAS FALLDORF

A married couple have been out shopping for hours when the wife realizes that her husband has disappeared. So she calls his cell phone.

"Where are you?!" she yells.

"Darling," he says, "do you remember that jewelry shop, the one where you saw that diamond necklace you loved? But I didn't have enough money at the time, so I said, 'Baby, I promise it'll be yours one day'?"

"Yes!" she shouts excitedly.

"Well, I'm in the bar next door."

—BONNIE TOWNSEND

My friend Garrick had the solution to his forgetting his wife's birthday and their wedding anniversary: He opened an account with a local florist and provided it with both dates as well as instructions to send flowers and a card signed "Your loving husband, Garrick." For a few years, it worked. Then one day, Garrick came home on their wedding anniversary. He saw the flowers on the dining room table and said, "What nice flowers. Where did you get them?"

—YEFIM M. BRODD

One morning shortly after we got married in our 60s, my husband and I were sitting on the bed putting on our socks and shoes. Out of the blue, he reached over and patted me on the knee, saying, "I am so glad we got married." He was being romantic, and I appreciated it.

"Me, too," I said.

He continued, "Do you have any idea how nice it is to open my dresser drawer and find my underwear and socks all folded nice and neat?"

—K.C.

"Your poor wife has told me so much about you."

A woman and her husband stop at a dentist's office.

"I need a tooth pulled right away," she says. "Don't bother with the Novocain; we're in a hurry."

"Which tooth do you want pulled?" asks the dentist.

The woman shoves her husband toward the dentist.

"Go ahead, dear. Show him your tooth."

—DENTALAFFAIRS.COM

After peering at myself in the mirror, I looked dolefully at my husband and complained, "I'm fat." Responding with the tact, sympathy, and carefully chosen words that I've come to expect, he said, "I'm fat too."

—BETH HARTZELL

I had just met my boyfriend's family for the first time. As I was leaving, his grandma gave me a hug and said it was wonderful to meet me. I said, "Thank you. It's nice to know I have your approval." To which she replied, "Oh, now, dear, just because we like you doesn't mean we approve."

—THECHIVE.COM

My wife and I were comparing notes the other day.

"I have a higher IQ, did better on my SATs, and make more money than you," she pointed out, clearly feeling that she was in the lead.

"Yeah, but when you step back and look at the big picture, I'm still ahead," I said.

She looked mystified. "How do you figure?"

"I married better," I replied.

—LOUIS RODOLICO

Who Wore It Worst?

∎

I describe my husband's style as "Is that what you're wearing?"
—@SIXFOOTCANDY

The worst part about breaking up right before Halloween is now I have to explain at every party why I'm dressed as half of a horse.
—@ROBFEE

"For sale," read the ad in our hospital's weekly newsletter, "sleeveless wedding gown, white, size 8, veil included. Worn once, by mistake."
—ELIZABETH EVANS

VALENTINE'S DAY GIFTS ARE SILLY. UNLESS ...

Love alone could make her day special, but why not add some bells and whistles?

By Robin McCauley

Please don't get me anything for Valentine's Day. I mean it. I don't need anything. I don't need you to give me material things to show me how much you love me. I know you love me. That's all that matters!

I mean, OK, if you really want to do something to show me you love me this Valentine's Day, you can just make me something. Handmade gifts are the best! I would love nothing more than a thoughtful handmade Tiffany diamond ring or card.

If you do make me a card, you don't have to write a love poem in it or anything like that. I don't need all that mushy stuff. Besides, not many words rhyme with my name, Robin. Maybe you could try "love." Dove ... glove ... in awe of ... I don't want to put words in your mouth.

I certainly don't need a pretty heart-shaped box of chocolates for Valentine's Day. You never know what is inside each piece, so you have to take a little bite out of all of them just to find the one you like—which is all of them. But no, I can't eat them anyway, because I'm trying to not eat sweets. Unless it's a special occasion.

Some women like getting adorable red or pink teddy bears for Valentine's Day. But not me! I can't even imagine where I would keep something like that, besides on my bed or on the couch or in the back window of my car or on my desk at work. Where would I put something like that?

I don't need to go out for a fancy dinner on Valentine's Day. Even if we wanted to get a table at a fancy restaurant for Valentine's Day, we wouldn't be able to now. It's too late. Right? Are you sure? Maybe we should call around.

You did? Oh. Well, there's no need to make a special romantic candlelit dinner for me at home.

I don't need a perfectly cooked filet mignon with mashed potatoes and asparagus—I'm fine with leftovers or frozen pizza. No Fuss is my middle name! For sure, don't worry about making a delicious creamy cheesecake with cherry topping for dessert. Cheesecake is hard to make. (There are really easy recipes online.)

Oh, and definitely don't get me red roses for Valentine's Day. Yuck! Who would want red roses? Pink roses are prettier. But as I said, please don't get them for me. They will just die anyway, and I would be able to really enjoy them for only a week or so—well, probably longer if I put an aspirin in the water. They would probably stay pretty for almost two weeks. Maybe three. But seriously, don't get me any.

And please don't even think about planning a surprise romantic Valentine's weekend getaway. I don't need to be whisked away for a fun trip to know that you love me. That would be just too much planning! How would I pack for a surprise trip? You would have to pack a suitcase for me, and then I would have to wear what you packed for me.

Like a bikini. Or my comfy flats that would make it easier to walk on the cobblestones in, say, Rome.

Or that blue sweater (in the third drawer on the right side of the dresser, beneath the gray shawl) to keep me warm during those chilly February nights in Paris.

But I know you, and I'm sure you are very sensible and know a surprise romantic trip would not be something I would enjoy at all.

It's a cruise, isn't it? You booked us on a romantic cruise?

"Looks like someone got lucky."

Done with dating sites. I'm now focusing on pizza delivery guys because at least I know they have a job, a car, and pizza.

—@LINDAINDISGUISE

As my wife and I prepared some of our belongings for a garage sale, I came across a painting. Looking at the back of it, I discovered that I had written, "To my beautiful wife on our fifth anniversary. I love you … Keith." Feeling nostalgic about a gift I'd given her 25 years earlier, I showed it to her, thinking we should rehang the picture. After gazing at my message for a few seconds, she replied, "You know, I think a black marker would cover over all that so that we could sell it."

—KEITH CHAMBERS

Wit & Wordplay: Speaking Metaphorically

■

You've got to date a lot of Volkswagens before you get to your Porsche.
—DEBBY ATKINSON

Arguing with your spouse is like trying to read a Terms of Use policy on the internet. In the end, you give up and go, "I agree."
—HERWAY.NET

Marriage is very difficult. It's like a 5,000-piece jigsaw puzzle, all sky.
—CATHY LADMAN

Before my daughter went on her first date, I sat her down and gave her "the talk."

"Sometimes, it's easy to get carried away when you're with a boy," I said. "Remember, a short moment of indiscretion could ruin your life."

"Don't worry," she said. "I don't plan on ruining my life until I get married."

—CYNDI LASALA

One lazy Sunday morning, as my wife and I were sitting around the breakfast table, I said, "When I die, I want you to sell all my stuff immediately."

She asked, "Now, why would you want me to do something like that?"

"I figure you'd eventually remarry, and I don't want some other jerk using my stuff."

She looked at me intently and said, "What makes you think I'd marry another jerk?"

—PLANETPROCTOR.COM

A lawyer told of being at the home of a wealthy divorced couple as they divvied up their possessions. The ex-husband had a wine collection worth millions and insisted on keeping it. The ex-wife had no objections, and the lawyer soon discovered why. As the movers carted up the collection, she noticed that the ex-wife had steamed off the labels from every single one of the wine bottles.

—URSULENE MCCAMLEY

I recently called to congratulate my parents on their 24th wedding anniversary.

"So, next year will be your 25th," I said to my stepmom. "Is that silver, wood, ruby, or what?"

"It's guts, I think," she replied.

—LYNETTE COMBS

My husband gave me a beautiful anniversary card that had lovely art and heartfelt verses. Wiping away a tear, I said, "This is the sweetest card I've ever received."

"Really?" he said, grinning broadly. "What does it say?"

—MARY WEBSTER

When a friend learned that I was seeing a man 15 years my junior, she accused me of being a cougar.

"Why not?" I said. "My last two husbands were cheetahs."

—ELIZABETH RYLAN

"I know how you love empty boxes."

A **man walks** into the street and hails a passing taxi.

"Perfect timing," he tells the driver as he climbs in the back seat. "You're just like Frank."

"Who's that?" asks the cabbie.

"Frank Fielding. He did everything right. Great tennis player, wonderful golfer, sang like Pavarotti."

"Sounds like quite a guy."

"Not only that, he remembered everyone's birthday, was a famed wine connoisseur, and could fix anything. And his wardrobe? Immaculate. He was the perfect man. No one could ever measure up to Frank."

"That's amazing. How'd you meet him?"

"Oh, I've never actually met Frank."

"Well, then—how do you know so much about him?"

The man let out a sigh and said, "I married his widow."

—STEPHANIE CAPLEN

My husband talks in his sleep. Unfortunately, he also snores, so I sometimes give him the wifely elbow. "What?!" he demanded one night, still mostly asleep. "Turn over—you're snoring," I said. He did as instructed and while doing so muttered, "That's nothing; you should hear my wife snore."

—KAREN BRUNGARDT

Spotted in the legal notices section of the Maryland-based *Daily Times*: Michael Ray Dipirro petitioned the circuit court to change his name to Michael Ray Forbes. His reason for doing so? "Ex-wife wants to keep my surname. She can have that too!"

—BARBARA BENTON

In the doghouse with my wife, I ordered her some flowers and told the florist that the card should read, "I'm sorry, I love you." Unfortunately, my instructions must not have been clear enough. When the flowers arrived, the card read, "I'm sorry I love you."

—MARK S. MAURER

My husband rolled over and open-mouth snored directly into my eyes last night if you're wondering how we keep the magic alive.

—@MARYFAIRYBOBERRY

Prayers for my husband, who, very tragically, got me nothing for our anniversary when I specifically told him I wanted nothing for our anniversary.

—@MOMMAJESSIEC

A new patient handed me her medical history form. Under past traumas, she had written: "Married twice."

—AMY WRIGHT BRILL

The DJ at my granddaughter's wedding polled the guests to see who had been married the longest. Since it turned out to be my husband and me, the DJ asked us, "What advice would you give to the newly married couple?" I said, "The three most important words in a marriage are, 'You're probably right.'" Everyone then looked expectantly at my husband.

"She's probably right," he said.

—BARBARA HANCOCK

A guy gets a ticket to the Super Bowl but finds he's in the nosebleed section. He spots an empty seat on the 50-yard line, runs down, and claims it.

"What a view!" he says to the elderly man seated next to him. "Why would anyone pass this up?"

"It's my wife's," says the older man. "We've gone to every Super Bowl since we were married, but she passed away."

"I'm so sorry. But couldn't you find a friend to come with you to the game?"

The older man shakes his head. "They're all at the funeral."

—HUMORPLANET.COM

"Why doesn't your mother like me?" a woman asks her boyfriend.

"Don't take it personally," he assures her. "She's never liked anyone I've dated. I once dated someone just like her, and that didn't work out at all."

"What happened?"

"My father couldn't stand her."

—JAMES RICHENS

My wife suffers the most when rosacea breaks out on my face—after all, she has to look at it. Still, she's always quick with a kiss and a hug, no matter how awful it gets. So I told her how thankful I was.

"No problem," she said. "I close my eyes."

—JIMMIE LYON HARRIS

Marriage is just your spouse perpetually standing in front of the kitchen drawer or cabinet you need to open.

—@COPYMAMA

After a health scare, I hugged my wife and whispered, "If something happens to me, the presents in my closet are yours." She whispered back, "If anything happens to you, everything in your closet is mine."

—DEAN SIMPSON

"After you acquire the power of speech, we need to talk."

"Oh, but it's fine for you to grade papers?"

There are women whose thoughtful husbands buy them flowers for no reason. And then there's me. One day I couldn't stand it any longer.

"Why don't you ever bring me flowers?" I asked.

"What's the point?" my husband said. "They die after about a week."

"So could you," I shot back, "but I still like having you around."

—KAY STRAYER

Ten years after we married, my wife and I were reminiscing about how we'd met in college.

"It was a good thing you winked at me," I said. "I was pretty shy, and I would never have found the nerve to ask you out if you hadn't encouraged me."

My wife responded, "What are you talking about? I don't wink at boys. I don't even know how to wink."

"Surely you must remember," I replied, incredulous. "I walked by the cafeteria, and you looked right at me and winked at me through the window."

She laughed. "I wasn't winking. I was having problems with my contact lenses!"

—BING BAYER

Every year for my birthday, my husband buys me a particular perfume that has a delicate floral scent that I especially love. This past year, with money tight, I told him not to bother getting me a gift. Instead, I asked that he handwrite a beautiful letter encapsulating our 25 years together. My husband leaned in, gently took my hand, and begged, "Can I

Because my wife and I are flea market dealers, we usually carry stacks of $1 bills. Not long ago, we had lunch at a restaurant and paid the check with singles. As our waitress collected the ones, she sized up my 70-year-old wife and said, "You had a good night dancing last night, huh?"

—ELLIOTT SMITH

please just buy you a bottle of perfume?"

—LISA COLLINS

Early in our romance, my fiancé and I were strolling hand in hand on a beautiful beach at sunset. My fiancé stopped, drew a heart in the sand, and inscribed our initials inside the heart. I was thoroughly charmed by the gesture and took a photo of his artwork. A few months later, we used that same picture on our wedding invitations.

Seeing the photo, Emily, the preteen daughter of a friend, exclaimed, "Wow! How did you ever find one with your initials on it?"

—CHRISTY G. SMITH

I LOVE BEING MARRIED. IT'S SO GREAT TO FIND THAT ONE SPECIAL PERSON YOU WANT TO ANNOY FOR THE REST OF YOUR LIFE.

—RITA RUDNER

My girlfriend and I worry about different things. One day, I was like, "What do you fear the most?" And she was like, "I fear you'll meet someone else, and you'll leave me, and I'll be all alone." And she was like, "What do you fear the most?" And I was like, "Bears."

—MIKE BIRBIGLIA

One thing I've learned from my last relationship is that if an argument starts with "What did you mean by that?" it's not going to end with "Now I know what you mean by that."

—DONALD GLOVER

Getting married is easy. Staying married is more difficult. Staying happily married for a lifetime should rank among the fine arts.

—ROBERTA FLACK

In Hollywood, an equitable divorce settlement means each party getting 50 percent of publicity.

—LAUREN BACALL

I have bad luck with women. A woman I was dating told me on the phone, "I have to go. There's a telemarketer on the other line."

—ZACH GALIFIANAKIS

I LIKE A WOMAN WITH A HEAD ON HER SHOULDERS. I HATE NECKS.

—STEVE MARTIN

A FLASH IN THE CANS

Her skirt had too much flirt.

By **Sky Gerspacher**

My life as an 11-year-old in Morganville, New York, in 1966 revolved around *Dark Shadows*, Snoopy and Linus, my homemade skateboard and, of course, *The Monkees*. I never missed an episode of that show. My best friend, Martha, liked Peter Tork, but for me, no one compared to Davy Jones.

My mother always did our weekly grocery shopping on Friday nights. I didn't usually go with her, but one Friday, feeling bored, I grudgingly agreed. I whined all the way there while she pretended not to hear me.

At the store, I wandered off through the aisles, hoping to find a cereal with a cool toy or mail-in offer, when I noticed a stock boy shelving cans of peaches. He wore bell bottoms under his store apron and a paisley button-down shirt. His brown hair was long—a classic Monkees cut. He stood up and I realized that he looked just like Davy Jones! My heart stopped.

I decided I would go to the bathroom, fix my hair, and walk by him again. I smoothed my dress, stood tall, and strolled past him, stopping to pretend to inspect some fruit cocktail.

I could see my mother chatting with another woman in the checkout line, her cart still full. I still had some time. I hurried to make a third pass by the Davy Jones look-alike. I just wanted him to notice me. Maybe he'd think I was cute. This time, I was delighted to see him look right at me, smiling broadly.

I blushed and smiled back.

My mother, meanwhile, was no longer chatting and instead was staring at me. In fact, she was waving frantically at me. I took one last look at the beautiful stock boy, then went to my mother, surprised by the look of concern on her face. As soon as I was close enough, she reached behind me and tugged on my skirt.

"Oh honey," she said, "you tucked the entire back of your dress into your underwear."

ON
THE
JOB

With a pile of 300 résumés on his desk and a need to pick someone quickly, my boss told me to make calls on the bottom 50 and toss the rest.

"Throw away 250 résumés?" I asked, shocked. "What if the best candidates are in there?"

"You have a point," he said. "But then again, I don't need people with bad luck around here."

—BECKY HOROWITZ

I have a PhD in acoustics, and I spent my career working as a research physicist. On my son's 11th birthday, we invited his sixth-grade class over to celebrate. I walked into the dining room just as my son was explaining to a classmate, whose father was a physician, "My dad's a doctor too, but not the kind that does anybody any good!"

—GERALD KINNISON

We asked prospective job applicants at our company to fill out a questionnaire. For the line "Choose one word to summarize your strongest professional attribute," one woman wrote, "I'm good at following instructions."

—THECLEVER.COM

I'm a letter carrier, and I occasionally run into people from my mail route at local establishments. One Sunday, my wife and I were shopping and, of course, I was not wearing my postal uniform. A young woman who lived on my route approached us in the dairy aisle.

She asked me, "Don't I know you from somewhere?"

I smiled and said, "Yes, ma'am. I'm your mailman, Frank."

With a broad grin, she replied, "Oh, I didn't recognize you with clothes on."

—FRANK MONGIELLO

I'm sorry, but I can't respond to your work email. I've taken my bra off for the night.

—@LIZHACKETT

When I worked at an employment agency, I was interviewing a candidate for an entry-level job. I read his application as we talked: name, address, year of graduation, and so on. Then I looked at what he had written next to the box that read "Position desired." "Near a window," it said.

—SONA DORAN IN THE NEW YORK TIMES

My paramedic team was called to an emergency. Before we took the patient to the hospital, I had a question for his wife.

"Does your husband have any cardiac problems?" I asked.

"Yes," she said with a note of concern. "His cardiologist just died."

—AARON WEBSTER

An utterly confused woman called our local fire station about getting a haircut.

"I'm sorry, you have the wrong number," I told her.

"Is this the salon near the fire station?" she asked, confused.

"No, it's not. This is the fire station."

"Oh! Are you cutting hair in there now?"

—KAREN STRAND

A coworker once showed up to the office in a white wedding dress with a crinoline, beading— the works. When our manager asked why she'd worn her wedding dress to the office, my coworker replied, "I was out of clean clothes and really didn't feel like doing laundry."

—LAUREN EMILY
ON FACEBOOK,
VIA BUZZFEED.COM

As the dentist labored over my teeth, he tried to make a bit of small talk.

"What do you do?" he asked.

"I'm a comedian," I answered.

"That's interesting," he replied. After a pause, he said, "Let's get an impression—"

"It's observational humor, actually," I interrupted. "I don't really do impressions."

When my coworker answered his phone, the confused woman on the other end asked, "Who is this?" "This is Steve. With whom did you wish to speak?" After a pause: "Did you just say whom?" "Yes, I did." The woman replied, "I have the wrong number," and hung up.

—GCFL.NET

The dentist quickly continued, "—of your teeth."

—MICHAEL BUZZELLI

I've never wanted to know the answer to anything bad enough to ask a question at a meeting that's running 30 minutes over time.

—@ABBYHASISSUES

Any job is a dream job if you fall asleep in meetings.

—@SOMADDYSMITH

Scene: a sporting goods store.
Customer: Do you have jogging shorts?
Me: We have running shorts. How fast were you planning on going?

—STEPHANIE CHAPMAN

At the end of the day, I parked my police van in front of the station house. My K-9 partner, Jake, was in the back barking, which caught the attention of a boy who was passing by.

"Is that a dog you have back there?" he asked.

"It sure is," I said.

"Wow," the boy continued, looking intrigued. "What did he do?"

—CLINT FORWARD

Now that my boyfriend is working from home, I've asked that we liven things up by pretending we're having an office affair.

—@FERNBRADY

I grew up above my father's tavern. When we were kids, we would race each other down the stairs every morning to sweep up the bar and find the change customers had dropped during the night. Years later, as an adult, I found out that my father would throw a few coins over the bar for us to find in the morning. It cost him only a dollar a day to have us fight to be the first one to clean the bar.

—ROD MOHAN

Overheard at a paint store:
Customer: How much for a gallon of that paint?
Clerk: Forty-two dollars.
Customer: Do you have a smaller gallon?

—LOUISE ARRUDA

Your salary is just your company's monthly subscription of you.

—@TWOTWEETSNOTICE

Nine real people who found their way to the perfect jobs:
- Les McBurney, formerly of the Sun Prairie, Wisconsin, fire department
- Andy Drinkwater, civil engineer for the Water Research Centre in England
- Faris Atchoo, internal medicine doctor in Waterford, Michigan
- Sara Blizzard, BBC weatherperson
- Dr. Joshua Butt, Australian gastroenterologist
- Dr. Ashley Seawright, Australian ophthalmologist
- Jim Beveridge, master blender at the Johnnie Walker distillery
- Tennys Sandgren, professional tennis player
- Todd Cutright, logger in Oregon

—BUZZFEED.COM

It's five o'clock somewhere," I say as I leave work at 9 a.m.

—@MICHAELSMARTGUY

*"What's this I hear about large quantities of ice, fish,
and small sea creatures being purchased by your department?"*

CLIENT FEEDBACK ON THE CREATION OF EARTH

In six days, God got a good start on Heaven and Earth.
But perfection might take some overtime.

By **Mike Lacher**

Hi, **God,** thanks so much for the latest round of work. Really coming together. A few notes:

1. Love the whole light thing but not totally sure about the naming system. Day and night are OK, but is there more we can do? Definitely need to nail this down ASAP.

2. Re: the "sky." Not feeling the color here. Would like something that pops more. Please send options.

3. Appreciate the work on the sea and land, but now there's way too much sea. The land is getting lost in it. In general, sea does not resonate well with our users. Was talking with the team, and the idea of having no sea at all came up. Thoughts?

4. Noticed you've covered the ground in vegetation bearing seeds according to their kind and trees bearing fruit according to their kind. Is this intentional? Thanks.

5. We're seeing only two great lights in the sky—a greater one for day and a lesser one for night. Thinking that maybe we weren't clear in the original briefing. Definitely need more than just two. Need to make this a memorable, high-value experience for our users. Please revisit slides 13 and 14 in the deck. Shout with questions.

6. Seas teeming with life is fine, but again, we need to reduce the sea. This is a deal breaker for us.

7. Are the winged birds final or placeholder? Some kind of weird stuff going on with those. Just want

to get clarification before giving more feedback.

8. Can we get more livestock and wild animals that move along the ground according to their kinds? Again, the passion points for our target users (slide 18) are land and animals. Whatever we can do to increase the amount of land will go a long way toward converting our users from passive consumers into brand evangelists.

9. Re: "mankind." Interesting take on the brief here. Big pain point is that mankind is coming across as largely made in your image. As you hopefully recall from the deck, our users are a diverse group (slide 27), and we definitely want to make them feel represented (slide 28). Afraid that if our users see fleshy bipedal mammals positioned as

"ruling over" the land and sea (if we're having sea), they might feel alienated and, again, less willing to convert into brand evangelists. Let's fast-track an alt version with mankind removed. Doable?

10. Please cut all the "be fruitful and multiply" stuff. We're a family brand, and this isn't a good fit.

11. Realize it's Saturday, and you were planning to be OOO tomorrow to admire your creation and everything, but I'm hoping you can keep rolling on this through the weekend. Need to get this in front of my exec team by EOD Monday. Will be around via e-mail and chat if anything comes up. Looking to you and your team for a big win here.

Thanks!
Mike

"It's amazing to think he started out in the lobby."

My friend has owned and operated a sewing machine shop for decades. Recently, a customer he hadn't seen in years came in to buy a new machine. Looking around the small shop and appearing a bit befuddled, she asked, "Whatever happened to that young man who used to work here?"

My friend smiled and said, "I got older."

—JAMES METZ

I realized just how long we've been working from home the day a package was delivered and my husband referred to the entrance of our house as "the lobby."

—KIM SCHAFER

My friend's dad, a professor, travels a lot for work. Once, when returning from a conference in Australia, he spotted a familiar-looking man but didn't know where he knew him from. So he confronted him.

Friend's Dad: You look familiar. Were you at the conference this week for international trade law?

Man: Uh, no, sorry. I wasn't.

FD: I definitely know you. Are you in law?

Man: No, I'm not.

FD: Well, I must have seen you at a conference somewhere. Which university are you associated with?

Man: I don't work at a university.

FD: Well, what's your name, at least?

Man: Matt Damon.

—NOT_A_FROG ON REDDIT.COM

Wit & Wordplay: Poetry Reading
■

WORKING-FROM-HOME HAIKU

Cherry blossoms fall
And gently float downriver
On my screen saver.

Is it Thursday? Or
Is it Friday? I don't know.
Everything's a blur.

Got a midday snack.
It's not fruit or healthy food.
Ho Hos are my shame.

—JOHN TOMKIW

A customer at our bookstore asked me, "Do you have the original book of *Romeo and Juliet*? My daughter needs it for school, and the only thing I can find in stores is the play."

—AUDRIE WESTON

Overheard—an associate to his employer: "Sorry I'm late. I got behind someone going the speed limit."

—MARY JO MARSH

Two coworkers of mine at the post office—a supervisor and a letter carrier—were always at each other's throats.

Recently, they were at it again, and this time it was a real barn burner of an argument. I walked in just in time to hear the supervisor deliver a crushing insult, or so he thought: "I've taught you everything I know, and you still don't know anything!"

—MICHAEL JOLLIE

New Hires

■

"That's a great place to work!" shouted my 16-year-old brother after coming home from the first day at his first job. "I get two weeks' paid vacation." "I'm so glad," said my mother. "Yeah," added John. "I can't wait to find out where they send me."

—STEPHANIE DIOCEDO

The new busboy was just 16, and because it was his first job, we were all impressed with how well he had done on his first day. Which is why we were surprised the next day when he didn't show up for his shift. Then, an hour late, he came running in, red-faced and breathless. "I'm sorry, I'm sorry," he said. "I forgot I had a job."

—JOY MASSEY

Signed up for my company's 401k but I'm nervous because I've never run that far before.

—@HUNTERMITCHEL14

The CEO of a large corporation was giving advice to a junior executive.

"I was young, married, and out of work," he lectured. "I took the last nickel I had and bought an apple. I polished it and sold it for a dime. The next day I bought two apples, polished them, and sold them for 10 cents each."

"I see," said the junior executive. "You kept reinvesting your money and grew a big business."

"No," said the CEO. "Then my wife's father died and left me an enormous fortune."

—JEWEL 99.3

The university where I teach has a policy that grades ending in 8 or 9 receive a "+" designation (78 is a C+, 89 is a B+, etc.). A student received his final grade and was adamant that I had left off the plus sign. I looked up the grade. The kid got a 58. I told him he had failed the course.

"I know," he said. "But I earned an F+, not an F."

"You want me to change this to an F+?" I asked. He said yes and left happy when I agreed.

—DAVID BARMAN

Virtual meetings are basically modern séances. "Elizabeth, are you here?" "Is anyone else with you?" "We can't see you. Can you hear us?"

—@MCCLELLANDSHANE

I called my local used bookstore to ask when it opens. The owner said, "Usually it's 11, but I'm in the middle of a lovers' quarrel, so today it's more like 12."

—@SARATARDIFF

I've never wanted to be the kind of successful that requires getting to an airport before 7 a.m.

—@TRESSIEMCPHD

"You have an incredible ability to cut through the noise
and get to the truth. We need you to stop that."

Like many attorneys, I have handwriting that's barely legible. After I scribbled instructions for one of my clients, he spent a minute trying to decipher what I'd written before declaring, "If I took this to a pharmacy, I bet I could have a prescription filled."
—DARRELL F. SMITH

We have a team member called Jimmy who has a habit of writing rude, dismissive messages to difficult customers. If they complain about Jimmy, we apologize and say he's been fired.

Of course, Jimmy is totally made up.
—@WORKI_LEAKS

While putting myself through college, I worked several summers as the rifle-range instructor at a Boy Scout camp. Since these were true rifles, seriousness and safety were the rule. On the first day of camp, after giving a stern-faced 20-minute lecture on correct shooting procedure, I turned to my campers with a smug sense of a job well done and asked whether there were any questions. At the ready to impart more knowledge, I called on the Scout in back with the raised hand. His question?

"Aren't those the same shoes you wore last year?"
—WAYNE SANDERS II

A customer walked into my clothing shop and asked to see the pants that were advertised in the paper that day.

"We don't have an ad in the paper today," I told her. She insisted I was wrong, so I got a copy of the paper, and we went through it, eventually landing on an ad for pants from another local store. Exasperated, the customer glared at me and said, "In my newspaper, the ad was for this store!"
—EDWARD OPPENHEIMER

On our commute to work, my husband stopped at a convenience store for coffee. As he got back into the car, I noticed something odd.

"Turn your head and look at me," I said. "You have a Q-tip sticking out of your ear."

As he pulled it out, he replied, "No wonder the guy in there asked me if I was getting good reception."
—LINDA TAULBEE

Before LinkedIn, I didn't know any strangers.
—@JOSHMALINA

I was ushering at a college graduation when I noticed a harried-looking woman carrying a fussy infant.

"Can I help you?" I asked.

"I can't believe there's no baby-changing station in the ladies room," she said.

"That's odd," I said. "There's one in the men's room."

"Good," she said, thrusting her baby at me. "You change him."

—ALFRED NAI

I finally make enough money to be able to put a television in each room of my home. I live in a studio apartment.

—LOUIS SAPIA

In his 2018 memoir, *Blowing the Bloody Doors Off*, Michael Caine describes a time he hailed a cab. After he got in and they drove off, he noticed the driver sizing him up in the mirror.

"Hey, I know you," the driver told the two-time Oscar winner.

"I nodded [in] encouragement," Caine writes. "I was hoping for something about how brilliant I'd been in *Batman Begins*. Instead: 'Didn't you used to be Michael Caine?'"

We were dining with my husband's colleague, a therapist, who told us that her 7-year-old daughter had recently asked, "Mommy, what's normal?"

Our friend gave a response that only a mother who's analyzed one too many patients could give: "Honey, normal is what people are before you get to know them."

—MARY-ANNE REED

My kindergarten student needed a glue stick, so I opened my supply cabinet to see what I had. "Wow! You have a lot of stuff!" he said. "You must make a lot of money. Where do you work, anyway?"

—CONNIE GAHM

Although desperate to find work, I passed on a job I found on an employment website. It was for a wastewater plant operator. Among the job requirements: "Must be able to swim."

—MICHAEL LEAMONS

I gave a presentation to a small town as part of my role with North Carolina's department of transportation. At the end of my talk, I asked whether there were any questions.

"Can we move the deer-crossing sign on the state-owned road?" asked a councilperson.

"Why?" I asked.

"That location isn't a safe place for the deer to cross."

—SUZANN RHODES

"I'm working from home today."

Our boss at the factory was a grizzled New Yorker with a management philosophy that harked back to the sweatshops of old. A shift without being cussed out multiple times was considered a win. But one day, after I spotted and corrected a problem with one of the machines, he offered me the highest compliment he could think of.

"Rich," he said, "you're stinking less at this job all the time."

—R.P.

My friend, an intern, was given $50 to get the chairman of the bank some lunch. Told to get himself something, he bought a shirt.

—STORIFY.COM

I was describing my job as an engineer to some middle schoolers when I mentioned that "one of my colleagues and I designed a medical instrument for measuring human muscle tone." Later, I added, "another colleague and I designed a system to allow merchants to print coupons at the cash register." Thinking that all this technical talk was confusing, I asked if there were any questions. There was one: "What's a colleague?"

—JAMES HAHN

Feeling ill, my supervisor went to a nearby doctor, who ordered an EKG. Upon reading the results, the doctor declared that my boss was suffering a cardiac arrest and called an ambulance to whisk him off to the hospital. There, doctors performed their own tests. But those came back negative. After some quick sleuthing, the problem was solved: The first doctor had read the EKG upside down.

—SUZANNE CLARKE

As manager of an electronics shop, I ordered a part, number 669, from the factory. When it arrived, I noticed they'd sent me part 699 instead. I fired off an angry letter and sent it back. A few days later I got the replacement. It was the same part, along with a note containing these four words: "Turn the box over."

—BECQUET.COM

A student stopped me in the hallway to say that she'd just learned that her mom had had me as a teacher. Then, after looking me up and down, she asked, "Did you used to be good-looking?"

—BOB ISITT

Essential **abbreviations** for your work emails:

- TL;DR—Too long; didn't read
- RS;TD—Read some; then deleted
- SS;IC—Saw subject; ignored completely
- TI;SS—Totally irrelevant; still sending
- DR;ARA—Didn't read; accidentally replied all
- SU;SDR—Saw urgent; still didn't read
- OV;SE—On vacation; stop emailing
- SOV;SSE—Still on vacation; seriously stop emailing
- WR;GF—Won't read; got fired
- WI;MS—Where is; my stapler

—MCSWEENEYS.NET

I own a dollhouse shop and quite frequently find myself trying to fit a dollhouse into a customer's car. One day, I was having trouble squeezing one into a back seat when the customer who'd bought it told me to step aside and hand it to her. Within seconds, she had fit that dollhouse into her car. Amazed, I asked her how she knew she could do it. She replied, "I'm an obstetrician."

—JULIE SILVESTER

Sadly, female airline pilots are still relatively rare. As a result, I'm often mistaken for a flight attendant, a ticket agent, or even a snack bar employee. One day, I was brushing my teeth in the restroom before a flight when a woman walked in.

"My sister would be so proud of you!" she declared. I figured her sister must also be in

A fellow commuter walked onto the train while talking on the phone to his mother. From what I could glean, he was trying to end the conversation, but she wasn't having it. I say that because the man finally declared in a loud, exasperated voice, "No, I don't want to talk to the dog!"

—JENNIFER PAULY

the airline business, so I smiled and asked why. The woman responded, "She's a dentist."

—GCFL.NET

I was in my patrol car by a blinking red light—the equivalent of a stop sign—when I watched an elderly man drive straight through without even slowing down. I quickly hit the siren and pulled him over.

"Why did you drive through the red light?" I asked him.

"I didn't," he said.

"I saw you."

He shook his head and explained, "I went through between the blinks."

—ROBERT MARKLIN

WORK EIGHT HOURS AND SLEEP EIGHT HOURS, AND MAKE SURE THEY ARE NOT THE SAME EIGHT HOURS.

—T. BOONE PICKENS

Anyone can do any amount of work, provided it isn't the work he is supposed to be doing at that moment.

—ROBERT BENCHLEY

It is more fun to be the painter than the paint.

—GEORGE CLOONEY

I do the best I can. Everything else is everybody else's problem.

—ALLISON JANNEY

Success is like sugar. It's too wonderful and it burns up very quickly. Failure is like corned beef hash. It takes a while to digest. But it stays with you.

—MEL BROOKS

Work is the greatest thing in the world, so we should always save some of it for tomorrow.

—DON HEROLD

I once saw a pigeon on the subway get off at the financial district, and all I could think was, that bird makes more money than me.

—JONNY SUN

Working at an unemployment office has to be a tense job, knowing that if you get fired, you still have to come in the next day.

—ADAM ROWE

IF WE'D KNOWN WE WERE GOING TO BE THE BEATLES, WE'D HAVE TRIED HARDER.

—GEORGE HARRISON

BACK WITH A BANG

She tried to get her head in the game.

By Denise Thiery

*T*o say that I had a bad case of nerves about re-entering the job market after my kids had grown would be the understatement of the century.

I was particularly uneasy about the computer. I knew how to turn one on, but I thought Excel was just another way to write "extra large." On my first day at my new job, the trainer sat down at the computer and began a rapid-fire demonstration of my duties. I stood at her shoulder and tried to keep my head above water in the tsunami of new terminology.

I always wondered if a person's brain could reach capacity. Might that be why I remember all the words to Chuck Berry's 1972 hit "My Ding-a-Ling" but can never remember where I parked the car? Now I know exactly what happens when my brain does reach capacity: It shuts down. I remember only three lucid thoughts before the cerebellum rebellion.

1. Is it getting hot in here, or is it just me? (I hate to ask this at my age because probably it is just me.)
2. This stuff is way over my head.
3. Gee, I feel weird.

Down I went; for the first time in my life, I fainted. I came to a few minutes later to find that the staff nurse was kneeling over me and a blood pressure cuff was wrapped around my arm. I figure I was minutes from being bundled into an ambulance by a couple of burly paramedics.

My first thought was "I hope somebody remembered to pull my skirt down." It's a miracle that I didn't crack my head open on the filing cabinet on the way down.

I don't know where I found the courage to return the next day, but I did my best to laugh it off. For weeks after, whenever my boss gave me a complicated task, I'd put my hand to my forehead dramatically and sigh, "I am feeling a bit woozy and lightheaded. I may swoon!"

ALL
IN THE
FAMILY

I'm lucky that my wife and mother are very close. I realized just how close the time I drove my mother to her doctor, which my wife usually does. When the doctor came into the room, my own dear mother introduced me as her "daughter-in-law's husband."

—ANDREW THOMPSON

When my friend and her 5-year-old daughter were shopping, the little girl picked out a dress that she loved. Her mother shook her head.

"That's way too expensive," she said.

Her daughter dutifully put back the dress, but as she did so, she grumbled, "Well, why did you have me if you can't afford me?"

—SHIRLEY NELSON

Feeling that I'd had a very productive day, I called my mother to brag.

"What's it like having an awesome daughter?" I asked her.

"I don't know," she replied. "Why don't you ask your grandmother?"

—SHERI MUELLER

My mom's angry with me for letting the dogs see their presents before tomorrow morning. Apparently I ruined their Christmas.

—@AKFARIZEL

My husband and I drove a thousand miles with our three young children to visit my parents. The reunion included my two brothers' bustling families, plus other friends and relatives. As we were piling into our van for the return trip, my father offered us a fistful of bills "to help with gas."

"You don't have to pay us to come see you!" my husband said.

"Oh, we're not paying you to come here," my mother quickly replied. "We're paying you to leave!"

—LYNDA SHENEFIELD

Our 5-year-old twins had been squabbling all day, and I'd finally had enough. Pulling them apart, I said, "How would you feel if Daddy and I argued like that?"

My son replied, "But you and Daddy chose each other. We had no choice."

—JANE LIVINGSTON

The 3-year-old insisted on helping me put all the laundry away. It's taken us only six hours and 10 minutes, and apparently pants go in the fridge now.
—@OUTSMARTEDMOMMY

A friend was due to give birth around the same time that her oldest daughter was due to give birth to her first baby. On the morning my friend went into labor, I happened to drive by her house, wondering what she'd had. A sign on the front porch gave me my answer: "It's an Uncle!"

—PAM LESTER

Our 25-year-old son moved back home with an eye toward socking away money to buy a condo. We never bothered asking how long he'd planned to stay, but I got a pretty good idea when I walked into his room recently. In the corner was a milk jug with a few coins in it and a label that read "Condo down payment."

—TERESITA CORCUERA

On the last night of our childbirth classes, our teacher took us to see the maternity center. We were gathered by the door when a mom, clearly in labor, and her nervous husband came rushing down the hall.

When he saw our group of pregnant women, he screamed, "Oh, my God. Look at the size of that line!"

—RACHEL ZEBOSKI

One day, I was trying to get my 7-year-old's attention. When he finally turned to me, I asked, "Didn't you hear me calling you?" He responded, "Not the first two times."

—REDDIT.COM

I am one of four boys and, true to stereotype, we fought. During one scuffle, Mom had had enough.

Me: Mom, you're invading my personal space.
Mom: Well, you came out of my personal space. That makes us even.

—@WVANDERTIE

She broke it up and demanded, "Who started this?" My brother Wes wheeled around, pointed at me, and cried, "He hit back first!"

—STEVE WALHOOD

On a fishing trip, my father told my 5-year-old brother that it was time he learned to bait his own hook, and then he left him alone to figure it out. When he returned, my dad found my brother holding a fishing hook in one hand and staring at a squirming worm in the other.

"What are you doing?" Dad asked.

My brother, nodding toward the worm, quietly answered, "I'm waiting for him to open his mouth."

—JOHN KASUN

When a squirrel slipped into my house, I did the logical thing: I panicked and called my father.

"How do you get a squirrel out of a basement?" I shrieked.

Dad advised me to leave a trail of peanut butter and crackers from the basement to the outside. It worked—the squirrel ate his way out of the house. Unfortunately, he passed another squirrel eating his way in.

—CORINNE STEVENS

My nephew and his friends picked my daughter and me up from the airport. For the next three hours, he had the radio cranked to 10.

"How can you talk with the music so loud?" I yelled over the din.

He hollered back, "We don't have to talk. We all know the same things."

—DELPHINE J. BUDREAU

Sibling Rivalry

■

Ours was a family of eight children, but only one boy. One day, I was complaining to my brother about having six annoying sisters. He wasn't having it. "What are you griping about?" he said. "I have seven!"

—DONNA AYER

When I was a boy, I had a disease that required me to eat dirt three times a day in order to survive. It's a good thing my older brother told me about it.

—ONELINEFUN.COM

My sister asked if I stole her sweater. Uh, yeah. Who else would've stolen it? You think a burglar broke in and was like, "Cute top!"

—@LAURENREEVES

My 3-year-old son: I don't know what I want to be when I grow up.

Me: You can be anything you want.

Son: (after a few seconds) I think I'll be a mother.

—MARY LAHL

Told my dad about a rough patch I went through mentally and he asked in a concerned voice whether I'd still managed to take my car in for routine maintenance.

—@MUSCLESKOALS

Rushing to get to the movies, my husband and I told the kids we had to leave "right now"—at which point our teenage daughter headed for the bathroom to apply makeup. Her dad yelled for her to get in the car immediately, and headed for the garage grumbling. On the way to the multiplex my husband glanced in the rearview mirror and caught our teen applying lipstick and blush, which produced the predictable lecture.

"Look at your mom," he said. "She didn't put on any makeup just to go sit in a dark movie theater."

From the back I heard, "Yeah, but Mom doesn't need makeup." My heart swelling with the compliment, I turned back to thank this sweet, wonderful daughter of mine just as she continued, "Nobody looks at her."

—DELORES BREWINGTON

Like all Americans, my family was ecstatic when Apollo 11 landed on the moon. Well, most of us. My blasé 6-year-old sister wondered, "What's the big deal about a man going to the moon when the cow jumped over it?"

—SANDRA DURKIN

While my mother was pregnant with me, my parents warned my 3-year-old brother not to get his heart set on either a brother or a sister, as they didn't know what I would be. He seemed to understand but added this caveat: "Well, if it's a dog, I hope it's a boxer."

—KATHLEEN O'HAGAN

When I met my brother's new father-in-law, he took my hand and said warmly, "You look just like your brother. He has a big nose too."

—MARIE BALL

I should have known better than to take my 4-year-old son shopping with me. I spent the entire time in the mall chasing after him. Finally, I'd had it.

"Do you want a stranger to take you?!" I scolded.

Thrilled, he yelled back, "Will he take me to the zoo?"

—KARLA PETERSILKA

One of my four nephews just brought me wine and said "Here's your Christmas juice," and now he's the one I'm leaving everything to.

—@KENDRAGARDEN

During a church social activity, I had to say a few words about myself. I mentioned that I was born in Quebec, that the first Côté had immigrated in 1635, and that I was a proud 10th-generation Canadian.

"I doubt anybody in this room can beat that," I boasted.

"I can!" came a voice from the back. Everyone turned around. It was my daughter.

—ALAIN CÔTÉ

After moving to the country, my 3-year-old daughter and I were often alone in our house. Because we lived in a rural area with no close neighbors, I wanted to make sure she would be able to call 911 in the event that something happened to me. After instructing her, I decided to test her: "OK, what would you do if you found me on the floor and you couldn't wake me up?" I could see her little brain working. To my surprise, she said, "I would go into the kitchen and eat anything I want."

—LAURA ALBRECHT

Like most dads, I imagine, I'd always assumed that my 3-year-old son looked up to me as he would a superhero. Until one day, that is, when, having picked him up from nursery school, I saw that we were about to miss our bus and decided to make a run for it. Once we were safely aboard, I noticed that my son was staring at me intensely with his big blue eyes.

"What's the matter?" I asked him, still out of breath.

Doc: *Your dad has been in a coma for nine days. We're running out of ideas.*
Me: *Let me try. (Goes to adjust thermostat)*
Dad: *(Opens one eye)*

—@KEETPOTATO

He leaned into my ear and whispered, "Daddy, I didn't know you could run."

—TANNI HAAS

I was in the third grade when the principal called me into his office.

"Did you and your brother leave the house at the same time this morning?" he asked.

"Yes," I answered.

"Well, it looks like Sam played hooky from school today."

I knew that wasn't true, and I told him so.

"He couldn't have. The only game he knows how to play is checkers!"

The principal smiled, patted me on the head, and sent me back to my classroom.

—M.J.C.

"It's good, but I don't know if it's refrigerator door good."

HOW I GREW FIVE MOTHERS

Whether colorful, delicate, or prickly, the mothers of this green-thumbed son make for one dazzling bouquet.

By **Marc Peyser**

When I tell my children a story about my mother, like how she used to share her cocktails with our golden retriever, or the time she tried to eat an entire pumpkin pie off the floor after I dropped it, or when I woke up in the middle of the night and caught her making a tooth fairy delivery in the nude, the kids always ask the same thing: Which mother are you talking about, Pop?

It's a fair question. After all, I've had five mothers.

Only one of them is my biological mother, of course. (She's the tooth fairy mom, and just for the record, she claims she wasn't wearing any clothes that night because she remembered her job only after going to bed, which she did naked, or so I learned on that I-wish-I-could-unsee-it occasion.)

I also have a mother-in-law, aka the pumpkin-pie eater. And thanks to my dad's can-do matrimonial motto—"If at first you don't succeed, tie, tie the knot again"—I've also been the recipient of three stepmothers. That's four wives for dear old Dad. Somehow, when they leave him, they stay attached to me. You should see all the I Heart Mom tattoos I have.

I'm not complaining, mind you. With multiple moms, you get multiple birthday cards and holiday presents, not to mention a deep bench of low-cost babysitters. On the other hand, you also get a bumper crop of opinions on how to raise your kids, what you should and shouldn't eat, and where you should spend your vacation. (The answer to the last one: at *her* house—not at one of the other mothers.)

Having this many moms has made me something of an expert on the species, and I mean *species* in the horticultural sense. As different as my mothers are, each one's personality bears a strong resemblance to a houseplant. (What, are you telling me you never noticed that about your mother?)

For instance, one of my moms is a total gardenia. She brightens whatever room she finds herself in, and she smells wonderful, but she also demands precise care. She needs lots of son (me) and requires immediate adjustments if her environment turns hostile. This explains her weekly SOS calls when she forgets her Wi-Fi password as well as her short temper with waiters, other drivers, customer service, and her cable remote.

I made the mistake of teaching her how to FaceTime on her iPhone so I could lend a virtual hand when possible. This was a very bad idea. I am now the frequent victim of the dreaded purse dial. Purse dialing is the mom equivalent of butt dialing, only she accidentally calls you when she's rooting around for her wallet or a tissue, usually when she's driving with her friends. It sounds like this: "*Snarfle rumble grbrrrr* her terrible face-lift? No wonder she *rumple frizzle clank* sugar daddy. Of course *jingle jangle* play mah-jongg. Can you drive ..." It's no use yelling

> ## With this many moms, I've become an expert on the species, and I mean that horticulturally.

"MOM! MOM!! I CAN HEAR YOU!!" When I'm lucky, her phone battery succumbs to an untimely death.

With one high-maintenance mom/houseplant, it's frankly a relief to have another mother who is a cactus. Sure, she pricks if I get too close—no gratuitous hugs here. She has also been known to forget my birthday. On the plus side, this mom hardly ever requires a drink (thank you, Alcoholics Anonymous) and can take any heat I throw at her. When one mother gets on my nerves (see gardenia, above), it's the stoic cactus I vent to.

Helpful in an entirely different way is my maternal dieffenbachia.

Dieffenbachias literally suck the impurities out of the air (get a few the next time you paint the house—your lungs will thank you). True to form, my dieffenbachia mom tidies up my kitchen and does the laundry without being asked. Like Mary Poppins, she's practically perfect in every way. In fact, she's almost too good. What's the point of having a mother if you can't carp about her just a little?

Without a doubt, my most entertaining mother is my Venus flytrap. She's exotic—actually, she's a showoff from her head to her toes. She used to go to a special pedicurist who would paint cartoons on her big toenails—X-rated cartoons. She thought they were hilarious; my fifth-grade teacher thought otherwise. (She would have loved Mom's naked tooth fairy trick.) My flytrap mother is naturally a die-hard carnivore, and the more unhealthy the meat, the better. If the word *nitrate* isn't on the label, she won't look at it. The last time we went grocery shopping, she loaded up her cart with hot dogs and cold cuts. When I suggested that the low-fat options in her chosen food groups would be marginally healthier, she barked, "Over my dead body!" Perhaps those preservatives will keep her fresh longer too.

Lastly, there's my aloe vera mother. She kisses boo-boos and makes them better, just like aloe gel can soothe a minor sunburn. *Fussy* isn't in her vocabulary—she's happy anywhere, indoors or out. She's the perfect mom to curl up with on the couch to watch an old movie, snug under the afghan she crocheted. She also makes a mean lasagna. Flytrap mom would kill for it, which is why I never divulge one mother's culinary gifts to the others. (Oops.)

I'm tempted to note that one anagram of *aloe vera* is *love area,* but that wouldn't be fair to my other mothers. They all create maternal love areas. Some may have unusual taste in food or nail decor, and all have species-specific maintenance needs, but they all love me despite my own peccadilloes. So thanks, Dad. You may have dubious taste in wives, but when it comes to moms, you sure know how to pick 'em.

As my two sons were climbing into the back seat of our car, Eric, 5, yelled, "I call the left side!"

That didn't sit well with Ron, 4.

"No, I want the left side!"

"I want the left side!"

"No, I want the left side!"

Intervening, I said, "Since Eric is older, he can have the left side."

"Thanks, Dad!" said Eric with a big smile. "Which side is left?"

—JOSH WESTON

My husband and I took our two boys fishing. My father was against it, claiming the boys were too young and hooks were dangerous. I told him he was being ridiculous and assured him that we would be careful. At the lake, our oldest son cast his line and hooked his little brother in the forehead, with the worm dangling across his nose.

"See, Mom?" he cried as we carefully removed the hook. "You should always listen to your parents."

—MICHELE CABLE

When my 4-year-old brother bolted from the yard for the umpteenth time, my worried parents put up a fence. Didn't work—Chris learned how to climb over it. So Mom came up with the idea of tying one end of a long rope to his belt loop and the other end to the fence. It worked splendidly, until Chris removed his pants and climbed over the fence.

—DONNA HOLTER

Wit & Wordplay:
Words of Advice
■

Be nice to your brother. You might need one of his kidneys one day.
—@COCOGURL86

Get married and have kids so that you can be woken up at 4:56 a.m. on a Saturday by someone asking what the opposite of *j* is.
—@CRAY_AT_HOME_MA

The older you get, the more holidays become about keeping your father off a ladder.
—@SHUTUPMIKEGINN

Being the youngest child means no matter how old you get, you're always going to be stuck in the middle seat of the car.
—@COCOTOOMAJIAN

theycantalk.com

"You can play dead all you want. We're still going to see my parents."

After having a brand-new car for all of one day, I came home from shopping with a fender bender. I told my 3-year-old granddaughter, Landree, not to tell Papa. Soon, here comes Papa—he had clearly looked in the garage. Not saying anything, he went back downstairs to his man cave. I asked Landree if she had told Papa on me.

"No, I didn't, Gigi!" she said emphatically.

"Well, what did you tell him?" I asked.

"I told him three times, 'Whatever you do, DON'T look in the garage, Papa!'"

—DIANNE KREICK

My 4-year-old niece Suzie was sitting with her mother and grandmother when out of the blue she said, "Mommy, you're so pretty." My sister pointed to our mother and said, "Honey, when I was your age, I thought my mom was so pretty too." Suzie responded, "When did you realize she wasn't?"

—JUDY NEWBERRY

My youngest granddaughter had just turned 5 when my wife asked whether she was being a good girl. After a deep sigh and a thoughtful pause, she responded, "You know, I'm doing the best I can."

—M.F.

After confirming her pregnancy, my friend told her 4-year-old daughter about the new brother or sister on the way. She made it clear that the baby's arrival would be quite a ways away. Her husband came home, and the family had dinner and discussed the good news. Finally, it was time for bed, and the little girl, suddenly very distressed, said to her mother, "I know you said it would be a long time until we got our baby, but this is just ridiculous."

—JANET SIMMONDS

I had to rethink where I ranked in my family's hierarchy when my sister and I found our dad holding court amid friends at a party.

"Oh, gentlemen," he said, pointing to my sister. "Let me introduce you to my daughter Terri. And this," he said, motioning to me, "is my daughter Terri's sister, Gayle."

—GAYLE SALTER

My husband brought the kids to a baseball game, so I woke them up at 2 a.m. to feed them candy. No way I'm losing the "favorite parent" battle.

—@CARBOSLY

Anyone with toddlers knows that trying to control them is like herding cats. So I was impressed by a parenting trick of my husband's.

Our 2-year-old bolted out of our van in a busy parking lot, but my husband, Bill, got him to stay put by shouting, "Hands on the van."

"Where'd you learn that?" I asked.

"From that TV show."

"*Supernanny*? *Nanny 911*?"

"No," he said. "*Cops*."

—CHERI DRAPER

When I get home from work, I like to relax with a magazine. My 3-year-old granddaughter, Olive, will often come and sit on my lap while I do so. One day, my daughter saw us together.

"What are you doing, Olive?" she asked.

Olive answered, "I'm hanging out with your dad."

—LEONARD ADAMS

At a baby shower for my first child, my 13-year-old brother let the excitement of the moment get the better of his emotions. He giddily announced to the guests, "I can't wait till the baby is born so I can find out whether I'm an uncle or an aunt!"

—TRINA BAMBERG

My 3-year-old grandson asked his mother whether his younger brother used to be in her stomach.

"Yes," she said.

"How did he get there?" he asked.

"I'll tell you when you're a little older."

"Just tell me this," he said, concerned. "Did you eat him?"

—PAT JEWELL

The first thing I did when I heard our great-granddaughter was born was to text my son: "You are a great uncle!" He texted me back immediately: "Thank you. What did I do?"

—PEGGY KLASSE

When you're a parent, you sleep and eat according to someone else's schedule. It's like being in jail, but you really love the warden.

—LEW SCHNEIDER

My 4-year-old just shut the bathroom door on me while I was inside and told me I was in jail. So I locked the door. I love this game.
—@KATEWHINEHALL

"Howard, I think the dog wants to go out."

WHEN YOU HAVE TEENAGERS, IT'S IMPORTANT TO HAVE A DOG SO THAT SOMEONE IN THE HOUSE IS HAPPY TO SEE YOU.

—NORA EPHRON

My mother had a great deal of trouble with me, but I think she enjoyed it.

—MARK TWAIN

I've been very lucky in my life in terms of people who are able to tolerate me.

—PATTON OSWALT

Happiness is having a large, caring, close-knit family in another city.

—GEORGE BURNS

Being a dad isn't just about eating a huge bag of gummy bears as your wife gives birth. It means being comfortable with the word *hero*.

—RYAN REYNOLDS

I want to thank my parents for somehow raising me to have confidence that is disproportionate with my looks and abilities.

—TINA FEY

When I was a kid my parents moved a lot, but I always found them.

—RODNEY DANGERFIELD

THE HIGHLIGHT OF MY CHILDHOOD WAS MAKING MY BROTHER LAUGH SO HARD THAT FOOD CAME OUT HIS NOSE.

—GARRISON KEILLOR

THE VIEW FROM ON HIGH

How many channels does this gizmo get?

By **Elizabeth Wiethorn**

My father, Ted, loved console TVs. I suspect it was because they were BIG. You felt that you were getting something for your money, even if it was an oversize box around an ordinary-size screen. In the 1980s, he found one (at an estate sale, no doubt, for an excellent price) that he parked facing the bed in the master bedroom—perfect for *The Tonight Show* viewing.

My mother, Ange, wasn't thrilled about this purchase of his. It worked for about three years. Then, one day, with a sizzle and pop, the screen went black. So Dad just plopped a slightly smaller console TV on top of it. Mom sighed. The second console died two years later.

Surely at this point we'd remove the carcasses and start anew? Oh, no. Mom and I watched in stunned silence as my brothers hoisted a third console on top of the others. The teetering tower skimmed the 10-foot ceiling, and we were under strict orders to give it wide berth when walking near it.

One night, in the middle of a Johnny Carson–Ed McMahon exchange, the top TV went silent, although the image shone on in all its Zenith-patented beauty.

Dad explained the complex viewing procedure: tune the top and bottom TVs to the same channel, control the volume with the bottom TV's remote, and regulate the picture with the top tier's clicker. Mom mastered the trick of juggling remotes.

It was a bittersweet day when Dad realized his tower of power posed too much of a risk. He got rid of the pile we'd dubbed the Eighth Wonder and life returned to normal—until Dad said he "found a guy" selling a console, "practically free"! He shut up when Mom sent three remotes sailing inches from his face.

BETTER
WITH
AGE

While visiting a retirement community, my wife and I decided to do some shopping and soon became separated.

"Excuse me," I said, approaching a clerk. "I'm looking for my wife. She has white hair and is wearing white shoes."

Gesturing around the store, the clerk responded, "Take your pick."

—ALBERT CUTINI

A widower and a widow attend their 70th class reunion, and a long-ago spark is rekindled. At the end of the night, he asks, "Will you marry me?"

"Yes, yes, I will!" she says enthusiastically.

The next morning, the widower wakes up troubled. Did she say yes or no? Confused, he calls her and asks, "Did you say yes or no to marrying me?"

"I said yes! And I'm glad you called, because I couldn't remember who had asked me."

—THECHATTANOOGAN .COM

I was on the phone with my 93-year-old brother in Wisconsin, and I told him that I thought it was time he paid someone to shovel snow for him. He suddenly grew indignant.

"Why should I pay someone to shovel?" he demanded. "I can get my son to do it. He's only 70!"

—DAVID GROESCHEL

I was having trouble with the idea of turning 30 and was oversensitive to any signs of advancing age. One day, I found a prominent gray hair in my bangs.

"Have you seen this?" I asked my husband, pointing to my forehead.

"What?" he asked. "The wrinkles?"

—WENDY LILLIE

Middle age: When you choose your cereal for the fiber, not the toy.

—@KITCHENSPROUT

During my 55th high school class reunion, I spotted an old friend.

"Bill!" I shouted. "You look exactly the same as you did in high school."

He nodded and said, "Now I know why I never got a date in high school."

—PATTY CHANDLEE

Middle age is when you recognize the classic rock songs that have been turned into elevator music.
—@BEANSANDBELLS

To celebrate my retirement, my wife and I dined with a friend we hadn't seen in years. The next day he sent us an email that included—I hope—an honest mistake: "How wonderful it was to see you both aging."

—LAWRENCE DUNHAM

When a storm blew in around our cruise ship, an older woman on deck struggled to hang on to her hat and keep her skirt from flaring up at the same time. My wife ran over to help.

"Should I hold your skirt down?" she asked.

"Forget about that," the woman yelled. "I've got an 85-year-old body, but this hat is brand-new."

—MIKE DREA

My husband, a big-time sports fan, was watching a football game with our grandchildren. He had just turned 75 and was feeling a little wistful.

"You know," he said to our grandson Nick, "it's not easy getting old. I guess I'm in the fourth quarter now."

"Don't worry, Grandpa," Nick said cheerily. "Maybe you'll go into overtime."

—EVELYN BREDLEAU

Both my fiancé and I are in our 40s, so I thought it was both amusing and touching when he proposed to me down on one knee.

"Are you serious?" I asked, laughing.

"Of course I'm serious," he said. "I'm on my bad knee."

—DEBORAH MASSEY

My body is like an old car. Every time I sneeze, cough, or sputter, either my radiator leaks or my exhaust backfires.

—@DESYMCKEE

Somehow, a friend and I got on the subject of age, which led him to ask how old I was.

"I'm 37," I said. He cocked his head and asked, "Is that all?"

—MARY CARRUTH

My 9-year-old daughter walked in while I was getting ready for work.

"What are you doing?" she asked.

"Just putting on my wrinkle cream," I answered.

"Oh," she said, walking away. "I thought they were natural."

—DEB FILLMAN

My husband and I were at our lawyer's office to sign our wills. After we'd reviewed them, our lawyer leaned over his desk with pen in hand and asked, "Now, who's going to go first?"

—LINDA HELM

"It's a postcard from your doctor. He says he'll be right with you."

My husband was bending over to tie my 3-year-old's shoes. That's when I noticed my son, Ben, staring at my husband's head. He gently touched the slightly thinning spot of hair and said in a concerned voice, "Daddy, you have a hole in your head. Does it hurt?" After a pause, I heard my husband's murmured reply: "Not physically."

—LAURIE GERHARDSTEIN

Soon after the offering plate had been passed around, a parishioner announced that someone had accidentally dropped in his or her hearing aid. There was a period of silence, followed by a congregant suggesting, "Maybe you should say that a little louder."

—STEVEN BROWNING

Wit & Wordplay: The Past Tense

■

I asked my 91-year-old father, "Dad, what were your good old days?" His thoughtful reply: "When I wasn't good, and I wasn't old."

—F.M.

I used to be able to pull all-nighters but now I can barely pull all-dayers.

—@WOLFYNEYDA

Even at age 88, my mother was vain about her looks. At a party an old friend exclaimed, "Edith, you haven't changed in 20 years!" "Oh," said Mom, horrified. "I hope I didn't look like this 20 years ago."

—JIM BRADING

Pointing to a 30-year-old picture of me, my 5-year-old granddaughter said, "Grandpa, next time you get a haircut, have them cut it like that picture." Problem is, I wasn't half bald then.

—ALLEN JOCHIM

For her 40th birthday, my wife said, "I'd love to be 10 again." So that Saturday, we had a heaping stack of chocolate-chip pancakes, her favorite childhood breakfast. Then we went to the playground and rode a merry-go-round. We finished the day with a banana split.

"So, did you enjoy being a kid for a day?" I asked.

"Of course," she said. "But when I said that I wanted to be 10 again, I was talking about my dress size."

—SEBASTIAN E., ON CLASSIFIED GUYS

While taking a clinical history from an elderly patient, I asked, "How's your love life?"

"I don't know," he said. "I'll ask my wife."

He got up, walked into the hallway where his wife was sitting, and shouted, "Hey, the doctor wants to know if we still have sex." His wife shouted back, "No, the only thing we have is Medicare and Blue Cross."

—SIVAPRASAD MADDURI

I asked my wife if she would still love me when I was old and wrinkled. She replied, "Of course I do."

—GORDON ROSE

I was taking my 50th birthday pretty well until I went to visit my family. I have two aunts living in different nursing homes. When I visited Aunt Alice, she blurted out, "Jennifer, you are getting gray."

"Well, yes," I admitted. "But I still feel young." I put the thought aside until I drove over to see my other aunt.

"You look so young and healthy," my Aunt Bernice gushed. "How do you do it? You have a youthful glow." I thanked her for the compliment but couldn't resist telling her about Aunt Alice's comment on my gray hair.

"Well, yes, it's true," Aunt Bernice acknowledged. "Alice was always blessed with better eyesight than I."

—JENNIFER CUMMINGS

Hanging up with my 90-year-old mother, I sighed, then said to my 96-year-old uncle, "She's so stubborn." He shook his head sympathetically and warned, "You're going to have trouble with her when she gets old."

—ANGIE KIEM

For over 40 years my grandfather put in long hours at his job, so I was more than a little curious about the way he filled his days since retirement.

"How has life changed?" I asked.

A man of few words, he replied, "Well, I get up in the morning with nothing to do, and I go to bed at night with it half-done."

—DENNIS LUNDBERG

There was no way I was going to allow myself to go gray while only in my 30s. So I dyed my hair. Later, I modeled the new look for my husband. "Well, do I look five years younger?" I asked. "No," he said. "But your hair does."

—STACY OATES

WHAT YOUR HEALTH PLAN IS TRYING TO TELL YOU

Your appointment may have been routine, but the billing process won't be.

By Serena Crawford

Dear Sir/ Madam/Spouse/ Dependent/ Dependent No. 2, This notice is to inform you that the procedure/treatment/service performed on January 3, 2022, is not covered under your health plan by reason code L0L.

Receiving an Explanation of Benefits showing that a service was not covered can be confusing and frustrating. We understand this and, to be fully transparent, are sending this letter to create even more confusion and frustration. Please refer to the following series of reason codes explaining why your problem cannot be covered.

PRE&PRE: This service requires preauthorization of the preauthorization.

PENPAL78: The Plan will not pay for this service until you mail forms back and forth with us seven or eight times (this is subject to change).

V0Cab: Because we're not sure what the word "maxillofacial" means.

TOS5UP: If there is a conflict between what is written in your Health Contract and what is written in your Benefit Handbook, we will flip a coin. If we don't like the outcome, we will flip again.

N1C3TRY: Procedures that involve the eyes, legs, nose, or throat are deemed to be investigational according to our criteria. What a marvelous mystery the human body can be!

N0D1CE: Even though you received services from a Participating Provider,

he hasn't been joining in of late. Also, we don't like his new mustache.

5ONG: Because the Taylor Swift song "Shake It Off" is stuck in our heads, and it's driving us crazy. Haters gonna hate, hate, hate.

DuMBA55: The Plan does not cover foreign objects in ears if the patient is an adult and the object is something stupid. Examples include (but are not limited to) a Cheerio, a Lego, a crayon, an hors d'oeuvre, a chess piece, and a gummy bear.

WhatTH3: Why, oh why, did you ever go to the doctor for this? Couldn't you have had Spouse/Dependent/Dependent No. 2 just get you an ice pack?

MATH4U: The Participating Provider/Network Not Available benefit after copay is equal to, less than, or greater than the fee allowance/coinsurance/out-of-pocket limit, or $ab^2x^4+bx^3+cx^2+dx+ad^2=0$.

LOL: LOL.

OOPSx2: Oh no—not again! Really? Didn't you learn your lesson the first time around?

If you have any questions or concerns about why we have not paid your claims, our staff is available and more than happy to converse with you Monday through Tuesday, 8 a.m. to 8:30 a.m., in Code, emojis, or pig Latin. We look forward to serving you by avoiding all of your health-care needs! Reminder: Isthay is otnay an illingbay!

Please retain for your records.

A **new patient** reported to his doctor and asked, "Doctor, do you think I'll live to be a ripe old age?"

The doctor asked, "Are you married?"

The patient said he wasn't.

"Do you smoke?"

"No."

"Do you drink?"

"Never."

"Do you follow a healthy diet?"

"Of course."

"Have you ever been in a hospital for treatment?"

"Not even once."

"Do you ever go out on the town and not get home until dawn?"

"I wouldn't do anything like that."

"Well," concluded the doctor, "you probably will live to be a ripe old age. But I wonder if it'll be worth it."

—MARTIEN STASSEN

Down Memory Lane

∎

Watching a TV show on couples prompted me to ask my wife of 60 years, "If you had it to do over again, would you marry me?" "You've asked me that before," she answered. "What'd you reply?" I asked. She said, "I don't remember."

—MILTON LIBMAN

I said to my daughter on the phone, "Your grandmother is getting more forgetful and more repetitive every day. If I ever get like that, you'll tell me, won't you?" My daughter replied, "Yes, Mom, you already told me this."

—GAYLE HAYS

Somebody will say, "Remember when so-and-so happened," and I'll say, "Jeez, I sure don't."

—DAVID LETTERMAN

"**My great-grandma** gave me this money," said my 3-year-old, happily clutching a $20 bill he'd gotten as a present.

"That's right, she did!" I said. "How did you know that?"

Pointing to Andrew Jackson's face in the middle, he said, "Because her picture is on it."

—ANDI OLSON

Being over 40 is like the movie *Speed*, but you can't drop below 600 mg of ibuprofen in your system.

—@SEAMUSSAID

"Highlight the battleship-gray."

I stopped referring to my parents as elderly after someone told me, "Well, they'd have to be now, wouldn't they?"

—SHARON SOLLARS

A nurse friend of mine took a 104-year-old patient for a walk in the hospital corridor. When she got him back to his room and sat him down, he took a deep breath and announced, "That was great! I don't feel a day over 100!"

—MARY CIPOLLONE

"Those frames are so flattering," I assured my sister. She had just gotten new glasses after 25 years and wasn't particularly happy with them.

"They're OK," she said, staring gloomily at herself in the mirror.

"Can you see better?"

"Yes, I can see better."

"So what's wrong?"

"Well, for one thing," she said, "I thought I was still cute."

—JUDEE NORTON

MEMORY IS OVERRATED

After a lifetime of memory lapses, Cathleen Schine
is happy her friends are finally catching up with her.
What were their names again?

By Cathleen Schine

Ever since I hit 50, everyone I know has begun to complain about word retrieval. My friends have started doing crossword puzzles and sudoku. For them, forgetfulness is an alarming new shift. But for me, nothing has changed. I have always lived in this land where everyone looks familiar but no one has a name.

I have no memory. I don't mean I suffer from dementia. I mean that from a very early age, I have lived in a vague, timeless valley ringed by towering mountains of what I have forgotten: monumental events and facts of my own life; friends' faces; eminent names; dates both historical and personal; brilliant performances on stage, screen, and street corners; engaging plots; and whole songbooks of lovely, lost melodies. In the quiet,

obscure landscape of my memory there are, of course, occasional intense, random details I vividly remember, which means my life is rich and full of surprises. And as my friends have begun to catch up, this forgetful life has become less lonely.

"That book ... the one about ... you know ...," I say.

"By what's his name?" Sarah says.

"No, the other one," Molly says.

"Oh, that book!" Sarah cries.

"That one, yes. That one!" I say.

"By her!" Molly says.

This conversation took place in a publisher's office a year or so ago: a writer, an editor, and an agent, all of us the same age, all of us nodding vigorous encouragement to the others, as if we were hunting dogs, huge-pawed puppies in the woods of middle-aged memory just learning to retrieve dead ducks, gingerly, in our big slobbery jaws. Scientists call this inability to recall a name TOT, or tip-of-the-tongue phenomenon. It has something to do with the anterior cingulate and prefrontal cortices. I'm sure there are scientific names for the memory challenges I live with, though few, I suspect, with such a jolly, colloquial ring as TOT.

A few years ago, I visited my high school boyfriend and his wife at their house. It was the first time I had seen him in years. He put on a blues CD.

"This is great," I said. "Who is it?"

He stared at me, clearly appalled. "Son House," he said, coaxingly. "You introduced me to his music."

Later that day, I remarked that it was odd that I had barely heard of the Grateful Dead, much less listened to their music, until one of my children made a joke about Deadheads.

Again, the dismayed look. Then, "You and I went to hear them in concert at the Fillmore East."

I know what you're thinking: It was the 1960s—those were the days— but no, sorry, not a druggy thing. A memory thing. Son House and the Grateful Dead just … slipped my mind. I like that expression. Things do seem to just slip from memory, lightly, unceremoniously, like socks dropping to the floor, unnoticed, when you transfer the laundry from the hamper to the washing machine.

A poor memory is in my blood, for I come from good, solid, forgetful stock. My mother, in particular, has a flair for absentmindedness, a complementary condition that has about it a pleasant, professorial air. My mother is my role model in this as in so many things, but when I'm honest with myself, I admit that I will never be able to even approximate her style, her talent, her … well, let's just say it: her genius. My mother has written condolence letters for

A poor memory is in my blood, for I come from good, solid, forgetful stock.

people still alive. She once parked the car four blocks from her house and, when she went to get it the next day, discovered it wasn't there. She notified the police. They searched for the stolen car for months. One afternoon, my mother was walking down Park Avenue and saw a blue Buick. Why, look at that, someone has a car that looks just like my old boat, she thought. My, my, look at all those parking tickets. There must be a hundred! There were a hundred—over three months' worth. She had parked the car at 89th Street, not at 91st Street. She had actually misplaced her enormous old baby blue Buick. But her finest hour, her magnum opus, the work she would always be remembered for in the annals of absentminded history—if the absentminded had annals and could remember what was in them—would be the day of

my cousin's high school graduation. My Aunt Lois had a party at her house in Massachusetts, and we drove up to be there. My mother, who was answering the door, held out her hand to one woman and said helpfully, "Hi! I'm my sister, Lois!"

No one can compete with an artist of that stature. I have spent many years, however, in my admittedly inferior apprenticeship. There are the mundane forays into forgetfulness, like arriving at the airport the day before (or after) my plane leaves.

And then there are the hideous moments of mortification. For many years, it pained and humiliated me to make three lunch dates with three people on the same day or to mistake the person sitting next to me at a dinner party for his famously despised rival.

Over the years, however, I have come to think memory is overrated.

To all of you fiftysomethings joining the ranks of the TOTsters, I want to say: There are advantages. For one thing, I can reread my favorite books without ever being sure what will happen next. And without a memory, one is forced to develop so many skills. You must be wily to hide your ignorance. (For you are very, very ignorant; how could you not be? You can't remember anything you've read or even seen on TV.) You must be charming to hide your rudeness. (For you are very, very rude; how could you not be? You cannot remember that you have met people, conversed with them, and listened to their intimate confessions.) You must be alert and discreet in order to avoid all these pitfalls, and you must be creative to find a way out when you do, inevitably, fall into the pit. It is exhausting to go through life with a terrible memory. But then, it is exhausting to go through life with an excellent memory.

"Mnemosyne, one must admit, has shown herself to be a very careless girl," Vladimir Nabokov wrote in *Speak, Memory*, his autobiography. How delightful to think of memory as an insouciant Greek maiden with long flowing locks and sparkling eyes, rather than a rusty machine that must be fed a constant diet of Japanese number puzzles. Mnemosyne was a titaness in Greek mythology who slept with Zeus for nine nights in a row. "Evening loosened her hair, after the god had removed his coat," Hölderlin wrote in a poem called "Mnemosyne." Nine Muses resulted. Mnemosyne was careless, indeed. You might say she forgot herself. With all of Western art as the result.

A lovely, reassuring notion, a balm for the forgetful. Just don't ask me about it tomorrow.

When I saw an elderly woman struggling to get her walker out of the car in the grocery store parking lot, I jumped into action. I grabbed the walker by the handles and tussled with it until it came out. Then I opened the collapsed legs, put them in the locked position, and placed the walker in front of her. Voilà!

"Thank you," she said. "But I was actually trying to put it back into the car."

—RICHARD PARISEAU

At the end of a crazy day, my husband and I collapsed on our bed and watched TV. As I made myself comfortable in the crook of his arm,

I said, "Know what's comforting? When I'm old and gray, I can lean on you, and you'll still feel young and strong. Isn't that wonderful?"

"For you, maybe," he said. "I get the old, shriveled lady."

—LISA LIPMAN

Me, in my teens: This radio station is playing my jams.

Me, in my 20s: This bar is playing my jams.

Me, in my 30s: This grocery store is playing my jams.

—@MOMMAJESSIEC

I'm 82 and I like to dress nicely whenever I go out. One morning, I donned a new peach-hued golf shirt and navy blue Bermudas. I thought I looked pretty sharp.

While I was standing in line at the deli counter, an attractive young woman approached me and asked, "Do you mind if I take a picture?" Surprised and flattered, I replied, "Of course not." As I struck a casual pose and gave her a wide smile, she took a picture of my flashy four-wheel walker.

"I've been looking for something like this for my grandfather," she said. "Thanks very much."

—LOUIS F. GERBER

I was feeling pretty creaky after hearing the TV reporter say, "To contact me, go to my Facebook page, follow me on Twitter, or try me the old-fashioned way—email."

—LEE EVANS

The other day I got carded at the liquor store. While I was taking out my ID, my old Blockbuster card fell out. The clerk shook his head, said "Never mind," and rang me up.

—ANDREA PRICE

"I believe the old lady was ahead of you."

I've never felt older than when my 9-year-old son said, "It must have been interesting to have been alive in the late 1900s."

—DWIGHT DUNWOODY

As my 40th birthday drew near, my husband, who is a year younger than me, was doing his best to rub it in. Trying to figure out what all the teasing was about, our young daughter asked me, "How old is Daddy?"

"He's 39," I told her.

"And how old will you be?"

"Forty," I said sadly.

"But Mommy," she exclaimed, "you're winning!"

—KELLEY MARTINEZ

A couple are getting ready for bed after a long day's work.

"I look in the mirror and I see an old lady," the woman says to her husband. "My face is all wrinkled, and I'm sagging and bagging all over. And look at this flab on my arms." Her husband is silent.

"Hey!" she says, turning to him. "Tell me something positive to make me feel better about myself."

"Well," he says, "your eyesight is still great."

—JEFFREY RAIFFE

A BRIEF HISTORY OF THE CAMPAIGN

ZIEGLER

FRONTLINE POSITIONS

STRATEGIC FALLBACK TO HIGHER GROUND

RETREAT

FULL-SCALE ROUT

TEMPORARY REINFORCEMENTS

PERMANENT INTERNATIONAL PEACEKEEPING FORCE

At a recent senior citizens function, I watched an older fellow ease his wife ahead of him in line.

"You ask for the tickets, dear," he told her. "You look older than I do."

Seeming to ignore his uncomplimentary remark, she stepped up to the counter.

"I'd like two tickets, please," she said loudly. "One for me, and one for my father."

—JEAN L. SCHAUER

Sometimes honesty isn't the best policy. A patient showed up at our medical office and asked, "You're Mary, aren't you?"

I smiled. "No, sorry, I'm not."

"Are you sure? You look just like someone I know named Mary."

"Well, I hope she's young and skinny."

"No," he said, settling into his chair. "She looks like you."

—JANICE GRUDOWSKI

Two regulars are sitting at a bar when one of them casually points to a couple of drunks across from them. "That's us in 10 years," he says. His friend takes a sip from his beer, sets it down on the bar, turns to his friend, and slurs, "That's a mirror."

—JACK ARZONICO

Not long after my grandfather bought my grandmother a pair of powerful— and very expensive— hearing aids, Grandma accidentally washed her hair with them in.

"Oh, that's just great," she said to me. "If your grandfather finds out that I damaged these hearing aids, I'll never hear the end of it."

—JERE SANDBERG

Curious when I found two black-and-white negatives in a drawer, I had them made into prints. I was pleasantly surprised to see they were of a younger, slimmer me taken on one of my first dates with my husband. When I showed him the prints,

his face lit up. "Wow! It's my old Plymouth."

—DONNA MARTIN

I was complaining to my father one day about the horrors of turning 50. He replied, "You know what's worse than turning 50? Having your kid turn 50." That shut me up.

—M.G.

After one glance at my updated driver's license photo, I said the first thing that came to mind: "Ugghhh!"

"What's wrong?" the DMV clerk asked.

"I look ancient in this picture."

"Well, look at the bright side: In five years, you'll love it."

—ANDREA RAITER

I KNEW I WAS GOING BALD WHEN I REALIZED IT WAS TAKING LONGER AND LONGER TO WASH MY FACE.

—HARRY HILL

I am older than fire, and twice as hot.

—CHER

Do you know what it's like being over 40? It's like being a day-old helium balloon. You're not in the sky anymore—and you're not quite on the floor.

—NOEL FIELDING

You can achieve your dreams at any age. Did you know that Harrison Ford at 30 was a carpenter? Vera Wang didn't design her first dress until she was 40. Even Captain Crunch joined the navy at 50.

—LESLIE JONES

I intend to live forever. So far, so good.

—STEVEN WRIGHT

I refuse to think of them as chin hairs. I think of them as stray eyebrows.

—JANETTE BARBER

I'm looking for a much smaller house and a much larger medicine cabinet.

—VIN SCULLY

One of the good things about getting older is you find you're more interesting than most of the people you meet.

—LEE MARVIN

DO YOU THINK I CARE WHAT YOUNGER GENERATIONS SAY ABOUT ME? I WILL WEAR THIS FANNY PACK.

—DIONNE WARWICK

CAREFUL WHAT YOU WISH FOR

This birthday gift just didn't cut it.

By Annette Goggin

For my 50th birthday, I wanted a vintage-style reel push mower. I drive a hybrid car, and those mowers spoke to both my concern for the environment and my need to exercise.

My birthday arrived and I got my wish. It was new and red and sleek—and it was over for me halfway through the yard the first time I used it.

The mower sat in the garage, and I was dogged by guilt every time I saw it. Each summer I made myself mow with it once to do penance for ever wanting the annoying thing.

After four years of this guilt, I knew it was time to move past my bad decision. I took a picture of the mower and posted it on Facebook.

"I am selling this Mascot Silent Cut 18 Deluxe Reel Mower for reasons that should be obvious already, but will soon become obvious to the lucky buyer," I wrote on the post.

"The mower hasn't been used much, but I felt like it took six years every time I mowed with it. I don't have a place for it in my garage or my life. Only contact me if you love the environment more than you love yourself. I just checked the price on the internet. I can do much better at $100. Despite my lack of marketing finesse, I do want to sell it."

Nobody wanted to buy the mower. I certainly wasn't surprised by that.

The week before Mother's Day, I got a great idea. I loaded up the mower and drove down Goose Heaven Road to my favorite greenhouse, which is owned by an Amish family.

I pulled up next to the building, opened the hatch on the Prius, showed Mr. Fisher the mower, and offered to make a trade.

Twenty minutes later, my car was fragrant with about $100 worth of flowers. As I was leaving, one of the young Fisher girls was mowing the lawn. Sometimes things work out.

HUMOR
IN UNIFORM

During World War II, my father often found himself stuck with KP duty. One day, convinced he could improve things, he told the head cook, "If you give me a paring knife, I could peel these potatoes faster." The cook turned slowly to my father and said, "Son, you're in the Army. You have plenty of time."

—JACK GIRARD

I knew my young wife was not up to speed with military protocol when we drove to the base commissary. Still, I was dismayed when she parked in the general's reserved parking space—something she mentioned she'd been doing for the past year. As a newly minted second lieutenant, I knew that was a big no-no. Even colonels couldn't park there, so I asked why she would do such a thing. She said, "I thought that the sign meant 'for anyone in general.'"

—ALFRED LUDWIG

When I was stationed in Naples with the U.S. Navy, my wife and I became parents of a baby girl, the first grandchild on both sides of the family. Soon after, my in-laws were out to dinner with another couple who were also new grandparents. My mother-in-law listened patiently as the other woman detailed what a joy it was babysitting for her new granddaughter. Not to be outdone, my mother-in-law said, "Well, my granddaughter is touring Europe."

—MARK NOVAK

My 6-year-old was playing with his toy soldiers, using a different voice for each one.

Soldier No. 1: I have a bazooka, and I make a big boom.

Soldier No. 2: I have a pistol that goes bang.

Soldier No. 3: I have a Swiffer, and I can make your house really clean.

That last soldier caught my attention. Taking a closer look, I discovered that Soldier No. 3 was holding a mine detector.

—DONNA LAWRENCE

My sister had her kindergarten class write to my nephew Nate and his Marine buddies serving in Afghanistan. Nate's favorite letter was this one: "Dear Marine, thank you for being in the Army."

—ANNE KOPP

During a combat medical training class, the topic was blast injuries. At one point, our very intimidating instructor pointed at me and said, "There's been a jeep explosion. What would you do if you came upon an injured man with a steering wheel embedded in his chest?" Nervous and unsure, I blurted out, "Drive him to the hospital?" For some reason, the rest of the room found this hilarious.

—GREG WHITE

A family friend was working at a gym on a naval base. To use the equipment, service members had to sign in with their name and rank. One time, an older gentleman wrote his rank as "R.A." Suspicious, our friend said, "Ahem—you look a little old to be a radioman's assistant." The gentleman smiled slightly before explaining, "That's 'rear admiral.'"

—NOTALWAYSRIGHT.COM

While I was attending the Army's Airborne School, an instructor demonstrated all the possible parachute malfunctions one might encounter. A student asked, "If we have a complete malfunction, how much time do we have to deploy our reserve parachutes?" Our instructor answered, "The rest of your life."

—NETFUNNY.COM

In the '50s, I was a clerk typist at our base headquarters in Verdun, France. We

Our base's Army Exchange Service carried a particular brand of underarm deodorant that I liked and bought for years. Then one day I couldn't find it. I asked an employee whether they still carried my deodorant. "No, we don't," she said. "It was always selling out, and I could never keep it in stock. So I quit ordering it."

—JERRY ROBERT RYAN

were a tough group. How tough? Our motto was "We never retreat, we just backspace."

—BILL ROBBINS

While standing watch in the Coast Guard station in Juneau, Alaska, I got a call from the Navy in the nearby city of Adak. They had lost contact with one of their planes, and they needed the Coast Guard to send an aircraft to go find it. I asked the man where the Navy aircraft had last been spotted so we could know where to search.

"I can't tell you," the Navy man said. "That's classified."

—ALFRED MILES

Since I grew up in the civilian world, I knew that my daughter's childhood as a military brat would be drastically different from my own. This became quite apparent one day when a playmate arrived and asked my daughter, "Wanna play commissary?"

—LORI A. BURDETTE

My medical unit kept me busy filing reports, many of which clearly didn't apply to us. Here's one example: "Personnel Trained for B-52 Weapons System." When the inspector general learned of this, he ordered us to submit a monthly "Report of Unnecessary Reports." Among the first reports to make that list: the "Report of Unnecessary Reports."

—SGT. RICHARD WEISER

Life Overseas

■

During a stint in Vietnam, I took my R & R nearby. After a night on the town, I grabbed a cab back to my hotel, but because of the language barrier I could not explain where that was. I remembered I had a pack of matches with the name and address of the hotel on it. I showed it to the driver and pointed to the match cover. A few minutes later, we arrived at our destination— the match factory.

—STEPHEN MURRAY

I was stationed in England with the Air Force when I went to a local barber. I told him that I had a date that night and asked for a very close shave. After working his magic, the barber exclaimed, "There you go, Yank. If you want it any closer than that, you'll have to bite 'em off from the inside."

—SENIOR MASTER SGT.
JOHN SOTOMAYOR (RET.)

Never volunteer! During basic training at Fort Leavenworth, our sergeant asked if anyone had "artistic" abilities. Having been an architectural draftsman in civilian life, I raised my hand. Then the sergeant announced that everyone would get a three-day pass ... except me. I would stay behind and neatly print each soldier's name onto his Army-issued underwear.

—STEVEN SILVER

"Well, if your allies said that about you then they're not your allies."

"That's my medal for having the most medals."

A SAILOR'S SAGA

His account of shipboard life went a bit overboard.

By **J. Wandres**

Strange as it may sound, I owe my writing career to a stint as a radio operator aboard the USS *Windham County* as it sailed to Japan in 1958.

To pass the time while I stood watch in the radio shack, I often typed letters to my brother. Feeling creative one night, I decided to use a Teletype machine to write about shipboard life.

I wrote all night, creating characters based on real crew members and my honest thoughts. They didn't come off as very heroic: I called one officer a "silly wimp, still wet behind the ears."

Before my watch ended, I tore off my 15-foot-long saga, rolled up a copy to send to my brother, kept one for myself, and deep-sixed the rest.

A week later, I was told to report to the wardroom for captain's mast, a disciplinary hearing for regulation violations. I was dumbfounded: What had I done wrong?

My chief officer, the division officer, the ship's executive officer, and the commanding officer were all present.

"Did you or did you not use the radio room Teletype for personal use to create this nonofficial document?" the captain asked, handing me a copy of my letter.

"Yessir," I croaked.

"And did you or did you not describe a certain ensign as a 'silly wimp, still wet behind the ears'?"

I nodded again as he and the officers tried to suppress smiles.

"Well, Wandres," he continued, "for violating Navy regulations, I have no choice but to restrict you to this ship until we reach Japan."

As the officers filed out, the captain ordered me to wait.

"Next time you use Teletype, make sure you turn off the transmitter," he said. "Every ship in our group read about the silly wimp.

"And by the way, that was the best account of shipboard life I've ever read."

During my teens, I was a squad leader at a military summer camp. We were required to wear our full uniform at all times, with no exceptions and no accessories or makeup allowed. One day as I inspected my team, I noticed that one of the female campers had exceptionally dark eyelids.

"Are you wearing eyeliner?" I asked.

"No!" she said defensively. Then, after a slight pause, "Why? Is it running?"

—ASHLEY HEAD

In San Diego to work with military linguists, my colleague and I checked into a hotel and ordered a 5 a.m. wake-up call. The next morning, the phone didn't ring until 5:30.

"You were supposed to call us at 5 a.m.!" I admonished the desk clerk on the other end of the line. "What if I had to close a million-dollar contract this morning? Your oversight would have cost me the deal!"

"Sir," he said calmly, "if you had to close that type of deal, I doubt you'd be staying in this type of hotel."

—YEFIM M. BRODD

My stepfather, a medic, was assigned a cubicle in the medical tent where the recruits came through. At one point, a nervous young man stopped in the entry of the cubicle. Pop pointed to a container a few feet away and told him, "Pee in that bottle." The young man asked, "From here?"

—SHIRLEY CLAYPOOL

On my grandfather's first day of boot camp, his drill sergeant brought the unit to attention and asked, "Is anyone here musically inclined?" Seeing an easy job in the offing, three soldiers, including Grandpa, raised their hands.

"Good," said the sergeant. "You three are going to move the commander's piano."

—BRANT DEICHMANN

On the heels of a big storm, our supervisor visited headquarters to be briefed. When the major had concluded his rundown, the supervisor pointed to the map, where colored pins indicated affected towns, generators, and so on. "What are the red pins at the top for?" he asked. "Those," said the major, "hold up the map."

—MAJ. RYAN JESTIN

HOW'S MY DRIVING?
1-555-5556

sing sand from quarries in Kuwait, Navy Seabees stationed in Al Jaber Air Base were building concrete aircraft parking ramps before the start of Operation Iraqi Freedom. When the quarries were closed temporarily, our stockpiles were exhausted in three days. The fourth day the following report was issued: "Kuwait has run out of sand."

—JOHN LAMB

took my 4-year-old great-grandson to the Leavenworth National Cemetery, where my husband is buried. While there, we heard the sound of a bugle.

"What's that?" asked Jeremiah.

"Taps. They play it at a soldier's burial," I explained.

A minute later came the honorary rifle salute. With eyes bugging out, Jeremiah asked in alarm, "Did they shoot him?!?"

—JACKI CAHILL

was assigned to a military intelligence unit as a temporary assistant. One day, a memo came around with instructions for all officers to read and initial. So I read and initialed. Days later, it came back with a note addressed to me: "You are not permanently assigned to this unit and are thus not an authorized signee. Please erase your initials and initial your erasure."

—NETFUNNY.COM

One of our jet fighters crashed in a sandstorm outside of Twentynine Palms Marine Base in California. Thankfully, no one was injured. I was assigned to help clean up the site by bagging the debris. My greatest challenge was simply getting the plastic bags opened amid all that wind. Luckily, our sergeant major offered me some sage advice.

"Tuttle," he said, "the trick is to be smarter than the bag."

—DON TUTTLE

I asked a scruffy-looking soldier if he'd shaved. He answered, "Yes, Top Sergeant." I got into his face and said, "OK, tomorrow I want you to stand closer to your razor."

—RALLYPOINT.COM

We were hanging out in our naval supply ship's lounge when the executive officer walked in. He took one look at the pilot sitting atop a table and blew a gasket.

"Don't sit on the table!" he barked. "Is that what you do when you're at home?"

"No, sir," said the pilot calmly. "But, then, we don't land helicopters on our roof, either."

—BRIAN LAVALLEY

I was instructing new recruits when an officer entered my classroom to observe and report on my teaching style. I thought I was on top of my game that day, but he was quite scrupulous, as evidenced by the fact that his written evaluation of me cited this issue: "Instructor

Home on leave from Iraq, my stepgrandson was showing off his abs. Not to be outdone, my husband thumped his prodigious stomach and bragged, "I still have my six-pack. It's just six inches deeper."

—K.H.

loses eye contact with class while writing on blackboard."

—HERM VAN LAAR

My mom was ex-Army, so during the holidays she and my dad would invite local Marines from Camp Pendleton over for dinner. One night, my sister came home from work at Kentucky Fried Chicken, still in her uniform. One of the Marines asked where she'd been.

"I've been to visit the colonel," my sister joked. The Marine looked confused.

"Colonel Sanders!" she explained.

"Sorry, ma'am," he said, "I don't know those higher-ups."

—STEVE CHIALES

OPERATION ORDER TO MY DEPLOYED HUSBAND

A military wife calls her husband back to home base.

By **Lori Volkman**

I. Situation

Civilian Home Group (CIVHOMGRU), West, has recently identified threat "military brain," aka MILBRAIN, adversely impacting deployed unit member DAD. MILBRAIN hinders open communication and prevents successful family reintegration. Known risk factors include round-the-clock exposure to military life, complicated by heightened compartmentalization and marked deadening of emotional receptors. As such, MILBRAIN in DAD requires immediate and ongoing resolution. Current unit is composed of:

- Civilian leader MOM
- Two rogue operatives known as Operative–1st Born and Operative–2nd Born
- DAD (deployed)

II. Mission

Prepare for reintegration of DAD into CIVHOMGRU, WEST by:

- Disintegration of MILBRAIN
- Introduction of counter-components DADBRAIN and HUSBANDBRAIN
- Reintroduction of concept "feel"
- Suppression of dictatorial hierarchy, oligarchy, and misogyny

Accomplish DAD homecoming with goal of fostering mental and emotional health of the family unit and avoiding any further loss of spousal consortium.

III. Execution

It is the intent of these maneuvers to prepare all members of the team for reintegration.

A. MOM, Operative–1st Born, and Operative–2nd Born will each practice elimination of all expectations related to basic everyday interactions. This will be accomplished by standing in front of a brick wall and attempting to engage it in conversation and elicit sympathy and/or compassion and attempting to get it to respond to external stimuli, touch, and/or tears.

B. DAD will increase situational awareness of social and nonverbal communications of others. This will be accomplished by standing in front of a mirror, making eye contact, and practicing HOME phrases such as "I'm sorry," "Let's get through this together," and "I understand what you're saying."

Upon completion of these basic maneuvers, DAD should progress to more advanced maneuvers such as SMILE, SMIRK, WINK, the HUBBA-HUBBA (two successive eyebrow raises), and NOD.

IV. Service Support

The critical supporting actors and services required to sustain the unit during this operation include:
- DAD's emotive alter ego, which has been suppressed for the past year
- MOM's noncontrolling alter ego, which has been suppressed for the past year
- Operative–1st Born and Operative–2nd Born's obedient alter egos, which have been suppressed for the past year

Upon reentry to the CIVHOMGRU, DAD should consider the following services and materials for future maneuvers DATE and WOO:
- Class I (subsistence): fine-dining establishments, wine bars, candlelight, or sunset-view venues
- Class II (individual equipment): razor, aftershave, deodorant, mouthwash, elbow cream, and civilian clothing
- Class III (major end items): flowers, jewelry, chocolate, handwritten notes or cards, and perfume

In preparation for such availability of services, DAD may spend time on the internet reviewing what these items look like, how they are utilized, and where they can be obtained.

V. Command and Control

Upon reintegration, MOM and DAD are expected to operate in a JOINT ENVIRONMENT for all operational and tactical maneuvers.

A. Command

The higher unit commander is GOD, not DAD. MOM, Operative–1st Born, and Operative–2nd Born are support, not subordinates, to DAD and will not respond favorably to orders unless delivered in the methods described herein and in the Basic Human Interaction and Common Courtesy Field Guide (BHICCFG).

B. Signals

This operation specifically prohibits use of the following signals: silence, thousand-mile stare, dirty looks, shark eyes, loss of consciousness during conversation, and drama (aka "pyrotechnics") of any kind.

Signed,
Mom, COMMANDER,
CIVHOMGRU, WEST

I was awakened late one night by a phone call from nearby Fort Meade, in Maryland.

Me: Hello?

Caller: Is Sgt. Rodrigues there?

Me: Sorry, you have the wrong number.

(Hang up. R-i-i-ing!)

Caller: Hello, Sgt. Rodrigues?

Me: You still have the wrong number.

Caller: Do you have his right number? There's a post recall and he has to go to work.

Me: No, I don't.

(Hang up. And ...)

Second Caller: Is Sgt. Rodrigues there?

Me: No. There's a post recall and he went to work.

Second Caller: OK. Thanks.

—HOWARD GRAVES

Safety is job one in the Air Force. Overstating the obvious is job two, as I discovered when crawling into my military-issue sleeping bag. The label read: "In case of an emergency, unzip and exit through the top."

—KEITH J. WALTERS

We were drilling with rifles for the first time when our master sergeant caught one of the ROTC cadets chewing gum. "Cadet!" he shouted. "I want you to run to the end of the field and throw your gum over the fence!" We were all slightly bemused when he came back still chewing gum but with no rifle.

—GUNAR GRUBAUMS

Pointing to a pan of chicken wings and legs disguised in the classic mess-hall manner, a young airman asked the mess sergeant, "What's for chow?"

"Air Force chicken," replied the sergeant. "You want wings or landing gear?"

—PAUL JAGGER

When the officer stopped in front of me during inspection, I sharply opened the chamber of my rifle and thrust it into his hands. He glanced into the chamber and looked surprised. Inside was a smashed cockroach. I figured this meant trouble, and it did. Nodding to the late bug, the officer announced, "Legs improperly aligned—six demerits."

—DENNIS DEPCIK

My 90-year-old dad was giving a talk at our local library about his World War II experiences. During the question-and-answer period, he was asked, "How did you know the war was over?"

He replied, "When they stopped shooting at me."

—LYNETTE COMBS

During a drill in college ROTC, our sergeant took umbrage with a fellow student's choice of footwear.

"Those are the worst shoes that I have ever seen!" the sergeant shouted. After a few more choice, unprintable words, he demanded of the student, "Now, what are you going to do about this situation?" The student timidly replied, "I'll mention it to my mother."

—HAROLD STUMP

In helicopter training at Fort Rucker, Alabama, I heard a radio transmission between an instructor and his student pilot. They were practicing hovering, a tricky maneuver.

"See if you can keep your helicopter inside the concrete boundary," the instructor said.

A few minutes later, he revised his request. "Hell, Candidate," he shouted, "just keep it in Alabama."

—ANTHONY D. LONG

My brother-in-law Dayton, a Marine Corps captain, was invited to a reception hosted by his commanding officer and his wife. Dayton was new to the base, so the CO's wife took it upon herself to introduce him to other officers. However, she was having trouble remembering his first name.

"It's Dayton," my brother-in-law said. "Just like the city in Ohio." That helped tremendously, because with the next person she introduced him to, she said, "I want you to meet Akron."

—JAN ALDERMAN

After my niece returned from her second tour in Iraq, I remarked on how beautiful her complexion looked.

"What do you use on your face to keep it so smooth?" I asked.

"Oh, nothing," she said. "I've been sandblasted."

—WANDA KALTREIDER

My family went to a minor league baseball game while I was stationed at the Marine base in Quantico, Virginia. My mother decided it would be a great idea to mail me a baseball cap signed by the team. "It's for my daughter who couldn't come," she explained to the players. "She's in Guantánamo."

—E.M.

Soon after arriving at basic training, we were marched to the base barbershop, where we were told we'd find a clipboard with our names on it.

"Next to your name," the sergeant said, "initial it." Everyone seemed OK with this order except for one confused recruit.

"Sergeant," he said, "what if we don't have any initials?"

—MATTHEW NAZARIAN

A friend paid my mother a visit. Later, I spoke with Mom and asked her how it went.

"I was very nervous," she said.

"Why?" I asked.

"Because he's a captain in the Air Force," she replied.

"Mom, I'm a captain in the Air Force, too."

"Yes," she said. "And you also make me nervous when you visit."

—COL. RICHARD A. VIRANT (RET.)

Wit & Wordplay: Asked and Answered

■

During inspection, a female officer asked our very nervous corporal what his first general order was. "Sir, this cadet's first general order is to take charge of this post and all government property in view, sir!" Excellent response, except for one detail. "Do I look like a ma'am or a sir?" the officer demanded. The startled corporal bellowed back, "Sir, you're a ma'am, sir!"

—MATT WAKEFIELD

As the general inspected our troops, he asked some of the Marines which outfit they were serving with. Ramrod straight, each would respond "Marine Air Group 36, sir" or "Second Marine Division, General." Then there was one young private. When the general asked "Which outfit are you in?" the Marine replied, "Dress blues, sir, with medals!"

—LT. COL. JOHN D. BRATTEN

In boot camp, we're trained to respond to a sergeant with such phrases as "Here, sergeant. Yes, sergeant. No, sergeant." Well, maybe not all of us. One day in formation, after the sergeant yelled one recruit's name, the recruit responded with a simple "Here!" "Here what, recruit?" the sergeant shouted back. The recruit answered, "Here I am!"

—RICHARD GURO

"I can defend this hill for another hour, but then I really need to get to the gym."

Anyone wanting to take pictures on our base's airfield needs a letter from public affairs, which happens to be me. One day, while out snapping photos, I was stopped by the military police, who asked for my letter from public affairs.

"But I am public affairs," I said.

"Without a letter from public affairs, we'll have to take your camera."

I did the only thing I could do: I pulled a notepad and pen from my bag and wrote a letter giving myself permission to take photos. The MPs read the letter, saluted, and left.

—JOE MACRI

Stationed in Iraq during Operation Desert Storm, I found myself in a world that had changed little since biblical times. With so few creature comforts available, packages from home containing cookies and canned goods were received with great anticipation. When I got a box from my sister, I happily tore into it, only to discover just how far from home I really was. She had filled it with packages of microwave popcorn.

—ROBERT T. SIMS
VIA GCFL.NET

When my daughter had her baby, I flew down to the naval air station in Kingsville, Texas, where her husband was stationed, to help. My first job was to figure out why there was no hot water. I found the water heater and soon discovered the problem—it was set too low. So I raised the temperature setting. My daughter was so impressed she bragged to her husband that I'd fixed the water heater.

"Well, I don't know anything about water heaters," he said. "I'm a jet engine mechanic."

—BETTIE W. CASHION

How did I know my new coworker was a veteran? When I heard him describe the impending birth of his first child as "when the baby has boots on the ground."

—DUSTIN THOMPSON

I admit it—I have a tendency to exaggerate, and I was afraid when I joined the Navy that my "creativity" might get me in trouble. But my fears were put to rest one day while getting into formation, which was determined by height. Now, I was shy of six feet tall, but when our drill sergeant called for all six-footers to line up, I stepped forward anyway. I instantly knew I was in the right outfit when I looked around. I was the tallest guy in line.

—GEORGE WALTER REAMY

THERE'S AN OLD SAYING ABOUT THOSE WHO FORGET HISTORY. I DON'T REMEMBER IT, BUT IT'S GOOD.

—STEPHEN COLBERT

I'm convinced my cockroaches have military training. I set off a roach bomb—they defused it.

—JAY LONDON

America is not perfect, but it's much better than anywhere else in the world.

—CATHERINE ZETA-JONES

I am easily satisfied with the very best.

—WINSTON CHURCHILL

I'm older than dirt, I've got more scars than Frankenstein, but I've learned a few things along the way.

—JOHN MCCAIN

It's hard to lead a cavalry charge if you think you look funny on a horse.

—ADLAI STEVENSON

One of the fondest expressions around is that we can't be the world's policeman. But guess who gets called when suddenly someone needs a cop.

—GEN. COLIN POWELL

Gentlemen, you can't fight in here! This is the War Room!

—DR. STRANGELOVE

Never interrupt your enemy when he is making a mistake.

—NAPOLEON BONAPARTE

In preparing for battle I have always found that plans are useless, but planning is indispensable.

—DWIGHT D. EISENHOWER

ANYONE CAN HOLD THE HELM WHEN THE SEA IS CALM.

—PUBLILIUS SYRUS

DROP AND GIVE ME KISSES

The fate of one unlucky Marine Corps recruit was sealed with a kiss.

By **Richard Strysick**

San Diego, California, 1959. Panic swept through my Marine Corps unit one sunny June afternoon. I was one of 61 recruits of Platoon 337 assembled outside our Quonset hut barracks, and it was time for our daily mail-call formation. The anticipation was high, as a letter from a family member—or better yet, one from a girlfriend—would do wonders for easing the stress of boot camp.

We lined up in formation, standing at attention. When your name was called, you yelled, "Here, sir," took one step backward, executed a smart right face, double-timed to the end of your row, made two quick left turns, and continued at double-time speed toward the drill instructor. The DI held the letter in front of himself, and you clamped the letter in your hands, continuing back to your place.

Everything was going fine until one recruit, Cliff, had the letter snatched back by the DI at the last second and was ordered to stop. On the back of the envelope was a bright red lipstick impression. Yep; Cliff's girlfriend had sealed the letter with a kiss.

The DI threw the letter on the ground. He then instructed Cliff to do push-ups and, when in the down position, to kiss the back of the envelope. Cliff was to keep this up until he opened the letter with a kiss.

We watched Cliff open his letter, amused but relieved that it hadn't happened to any of us. That night during the time allotted for letter writing, all of us wrote to our girlfriends: Under no circumstances are you to write anything other than your name and address on that envelope! I wrote my letter to my girlfriend, Sue Graefe of Sheboygan, Wisconsin, now my wife of 53 years.

JUST
FOR
FUN

So a guy walks into a bar with a pair of jumper cables hanging around his neck. The bartender gives him a look and says gruffly, "All right, pal, I'll let you stay, but don't start anything."

—SCOTT HOFFMAN

Sitting in a hospital waiting room, I watched a woman helping her son finish a crossword puzzle.

"Mom," he asked, "what fits here?"

"It's man's best friend," she hinted.

The boy thought for a second, then guessed, "Duct tape?"

—CAEL JACOBS

A farmer was helping one of his cows give birth when he noticed his 4-year-old son standing at the fence, watching. Thinking it might be the perfect time to broach the whole birds-and-the-bees topic, he asked, "Well, son, do you have any questions?"

"Just one," gasped the wide-eyed boy. "How fast was that calf going when he hit the cow?"

—RANCHERS.NET

The police arrested a suspicious man selling "secret formula" tablets that he claimed gave eternal youth. To the officers' surprise, it was actually the fifth time he'd been caught for committing the same medical fraud. He had also been arrested in 1794, 1856, 1928, and 1983.

—INVESTORSHUB
.ADVFN.COM

A poodle and a collie are walking down the street when the poodle suddenly confides to his friend.

"My life is a mess," he says. "My owner is mean, my girlfriend is having an affair with a German shepherd, and I'm as nervous as a hamster."

"Why don't you go see a psychiatrist?" suggests the collie.

"I can't," says the poodle. "I'm not allowed on the couch."

—GUNDOGMAG.COM

Did you hear about the scientist who crossed a carrier pigeon with a woodpecker?

He got a bird that not only delivers messages to their destination but also knocks on the door when it gets there.

—JOHN R. FOX

Two men are hiking through the woods when one of them cries out, "Snake! Run!" His companion laughs at him. "Oh, relax. It's only a baby," he says. "Don't you hear the rattle?"

—STEVE SMITH

As the customer approaches the general store, he notices this large sign on the door: DANGER! BEWARE OF DOG! He carefully enters the store, but once inside all he sees is a fat old hound soundly asleep on the floor.

"Is that the dog folks are supposed to beware of?" he asks the store owner.

"Yep, that's him," the owner says.

"He doesn't look very dangerous to me," the customer says. "Why would you post that sign?"

"Because," says the owner, "before I posted that sign, people kept tripping over him."

—PETCENTRAL.CHEWY .COM

A scrawny little fellow showed up at the lumber camp looking for work.

"Just give me a chance to show you what I can do," he said to the head lumberjack.

"All right," said the boss. "Take your ax and cut down that redwood tree over there."

Five minutes later the skinny guy was back.

"I cut it down," he said, "and split it up into lumber."

The boss couldn't believe his eyes. "Where did you learn to cut trees like that?"

"The Sahara," the man answered.

"The Sahara Desert?"

"Desert? Oh sure, that's what they call it *now*!"

—KUMIKO YOSHIDA

The world's worst actor is performing *Hamlet*. He's so awful that during the "To be or not to be" speech, the audience boos and throws things. Finally, the actor has enough. He steps to the edge of the stage and says, "Look, folks, I didn't write this junk."

—A PRAIRIE HOME COMPANION

A garden gnome is busy destroying plants when suddenly a house cat appears.

"What are you?" asks the cat.

"I'm a gnome. I steal food from humans, I kill their plants, and I raise a ruckus at night to drive them up the wall. I just love mischief! And what, may I ask, are you?"

The cat thinks for a moment and says, "I guess I'm a gnome."

—NEWBLOGGYCAT.COM

A woman is in an exclusive pet store looking to buy a sweater for her dog. After witnessing much hemming and hawing and the scrutinizing of the size of each item, the salesperson finally pipes in. "Why don't you bring the dog in for a fitting?" he says. "I can't do that," the customer says. "The sweater is a surprise."

—BEINGHUMAN.COM

Two friends were beginning a game of golf. The first man stepped up to the tee, hit the ball, and got a hole in one. The other man said, "Great. Now I'll take my practice swing, and then we'll start the game."

—EDWARD W. STRICKLER

I was dining with the actor Ben Chapman, who had starred in a horror film in the 1950s. Bennie got a little drunk and loud and ended up getting kicked out by the maître d'.

"Sir," I said, "do you know who you are ejecting? This is the Creature from the Black Lagoon!"

The maître d' snarled, "I don't care where he's from—he's gotta leave!"

—M.C. GWYNNE,
IN PLANET PROCTOR
NEWSLETTER

After standing in line at the DMV for what felt like eons, my brother finally got to the counter. As the clerk typed his name into the computer, she said, "That's odd."

"What's wrong?" James asked.

"My computer says you're deceased."

Surveying his surroundings, James muttered, "Great. I died and went to hell."

—FAE BUNDERSON

Fred **Astaire** and Ginger Rogers were dining in New York. Ginger was resplendent in a ball gown and pearls, and Fred also sported evening wear. But the meal was marred when the waiter bringing their desserts tripped and covered Fred from head to toe in treacle sponge.

"I'm terribly sorry," said the waiter.

"So you should be," replied Fred. "Thanks to you, I've pudding on my top hat, pudding on my white tie, pudding on my tails."

—GEORGE KLOSS

As a man steps off the curb to cross the street, a car careens around the corner and heads straight for him. The alarmed man tries to hurry, but the car changes lanes and is still coming at him. So he turns to go back to the sidewalk. Too late—the car changes lanes again. Panicked, the man freezes in the middle of the road, and just as the car is about to hit him, it comes to a screeching halt. The driver's window rolls down, and a squirrel pokes his head out.

"See?" he says. "It's not as easy as it looks!"

—RICHARD MOULTON

Eight comedians are sitting together in a bar telling jokes.

"Twelve!" one of them says. The others burst out laughing.

"Four!" shouts another, again cracking up the others.

When a third hollers "Twenty-two!!!" forget it, they're all guffawing. Except the bartender.

"What's so funny about just calling out numbers?" he says.

I was singing along with the radio as it played the Beatles song "Lucy in the Sky with Diamonds." As I sang the lyric "the girl with kaleidoscope eyes," my husband interrupted. "Is that what he's singing?" he asked. "All these years, I thought it was 'the girl with colitis goes by.'"

—LYNETTE HARRELL

"We all know the same jokes, so we gave them numbers," says the first comedian. "To save time, we just shout out the numbers."

The bartender decides to try it and yells "Six!" A dead silence descends upon the bar.

"Why didn't I get any laughs?" he asks.

The comedians shrug. "You didn't tell it right."

—FRIARSCLUB.COM

Spotted on the back of an Amish horse-drawn carriage in Pennsylvania, this handwritten sign: "Energy efficient vehicle: Runs on oats and grass. Caution: Do not step in exhaust."

—WILSON FRAMPTON

I was standing on the subway when the woman seated in front of me got up. As she exited, I spied a glove where she had been sitting. Grabbing it, I ran to the door, shouted, "Miss, your glove!" and tossed it to her on the platform just as the doors slammed shut. Pleased with my good deed, I sat back down. That's when I felt a tap on my shoulder from the woman sitting next to me.

"That," she said, "was my glove."

—JUDITH TEDINO

The black lacquer stand holding his prized samurai swords was dusty, so my husband left our cleaning lady a note reading "Check out my swords." That evening, he found the stand just as dirty as before but with this appended to his note: "Nice swords."

—ELEONORE BODE-LEMMING

A pigeon was anxiously pacing up and down the street when he saw his friend hop up on the curb.

"Where have you been?" he asked. "I've been waiting here for hours."

"Sorry I'm late," his friend replied. "It was just such a nice day, I thought I'd walk."

—THAYERBIRDING.COM

Wit & Wordplay: Colorful Language

■

It's late at night and a man is getting ready for bed when he hears a knock on his door. He opens it and looks down to see a snail on the front step. "I'd like to talk to you about buying some magazine subscriptions," says the snail. Furious at being disturbed, the man rears back, kicks the snail as hard as he can, and storms off to bed. Two years later there comes another knock. The man answers and again finds the snail, who looks up and says, "What the @#$% was that all about?"

—FROM A CARNIVAL OF SNACKERY BY DAVID SEDARIS

A priest buys a lawn mower at a yard sale. Once he arrives back home, he pulls on the starter rope a few times with no results. He storms back to the yard sale and tells the previous owner, "I can't get the mower to start!" "That's because you have to curse to get it started," says the man. "I'm a man of the cloth. I don't even remember how to curse!" "You keep pulling on that rope, and it'll come back to you."

—ROSE MATTIX

A doctor answered the phone and heard the familiar voice of a colleague on the other end of the line say, "We need a fourth for poker."

"I'll be right over," the doctor answered.

As he was putting on his coat, his wife asked, "Is it serious?"

"Oh, yes," the doctor answered gravely. "In fact, there are three doctors there already."

—DOROTHEA KENT

Two buddies were watching the game when one turned to his friend and said, "You won't believe it. All last night I kept dreaming of a horse and the number five. So I went to the track, put $500 on the fifth horse in the fifth race, and you won't believe what happened."

"Did he win?"

"Nah," the guy said. "He came in fifth."

—LUIS ANDRE

The village blacksmith finally found an apprentice willing to work long, hard hours at the forge. The blacksmith instructed the boy, "When I take the shoe out of the fire, I'll lay it on the anvil, and when I nod my head, you hit it with this hammer." The apprentice did just as he was told. Now he's the village blacksmith.

—VALLEYBUGLER.COM

WELCOME TO OUR CORN MAZE!

This year, autumn-loving visitors might be better off opting for the pumpkin patch.

By **Colin Nissan**

Is it difficult to get out of the maze? Stretching a mile and a half, the Honey Pot Hills Orchard maze is one of the largest in New England! It can certainly be challenging, but that's the fun!

What's the average time it takes to exit the maze? It ranges. We've had some lucky folks find their way out in under an hour; others are still in there, as far as we know.

What if I don't make it out before Honey Pot Hills closes? If you've lost all hope of finding a path of egress, we strongly suggest building a shelter and a fire before nightfall. The temperature really drops inside the maze (*Brr!*) and, from what we understand, securing a campsite can often be quite contentious.

Is there crime inside the maze? We wish we were immune to typical corn-maze problems here at Honey Pot Hills, but unfortunately we aren't. Crime is a persistent issue, particularly theft, assault, and kidnapping. While we're doing everything we can to contain these threats, please be vigilant and don't invite conflict. Keep cellphones, wallets, and candy apples out of sight at all times.

Can I bring in food and beverages? No outside food or beverages are allowed inside the maze, but our concession stand just outside of the entrance has great fall treats and drinks. There are also indigenous animals such as mice and snakes that you are welcome to hunt for survival.

What if I need medical attention? We air-drop medical supplies into the maze twice a week, but please don't hoard them. One consequence of the airdrops is the formation of a maze black market—one that also deals in food, blankets, phone accessories, toiletries, and narcotics.

I heard that there are people who find the exit but choose not to leave. Some folks, after spending prolonged periods of time in the maze, do experience the feeling that they belong there. Life inside makes sense to them in a way that their lives outside never did. It doesn't take long for awareness of their former selves to fade away, at which point they submit fully to the maze and are reborn.

Do you guys have hayrides? Sure do!

Do children need to be accompanied by adults in the maze? Yes.

But I saw some kids without adults. It's likely that their parents passed away in the maze, leaving the so-called maze orphans behind. You may also come across maze babies—children who were born inside the maze and have never actually seen the outside world.

How's literacy inside the maze? Regrettably, illiteracy rates have soared over the past few autumns. We're combating this problem by air-dropping books and school supplies. If you are a teacher who wants to donate time, we can drop you in as well. Even a few hours would help.

What if I've amassed gambling debts inside that I can't pay off? You wouldn't be alone. A gambling syndicate has plagued the maze in recent years. You won't have to walk far to see a crowd huddled around a game of Niblitz, a popular dice game that uses dried corn kernels.

Is it true there are warlords inside? Boy, are there. They've developed considerable followings. The most notorious of these is called the Crow. He patrols the labyrinth with a screeching murder of leashed crows. He has a fiercely loyal army of mazegoers to whom he provides a high level of protection.

Do you have Wi-Fi? You bet! The password is CIDER99. All caps.

Three male dogs are walking down the street when they see a beautiful female poodle. They all scramble to reach her first but end up arriving in front of her at the same time. Aware of her obvious effect on the suitors, she tells them, "The first one who uses the words *liver* and *cheese* together in an imaginative sentence can go out with me."

"I love liver and cheese!" the golden retriever blurts out.

"Oh, how childish," says the poodle. The Labrador tries next.

"Um. I hate liver and cheese?"

"My, my," says the poodle. "I guess it's hopeless." She then turns to the last of the three dogs and says, "How about you, little guy? What have you got to say for yourself?"

The Yorkie, tiny in stature but big in finesse, gives her a smile and a sly wink, turns to the other dogs, and says, "Liver alone—cheese mine!"

—PLANET PROCTOR

Vacationing in Arizona, a group of British tourists spots a cowboy lying by the side of the road with his ear to the ground.

"What's going on?" they ask.

"Two horses—one gray, one chestnut— are pulling a wagon carrying two men," the cowboy says. "One man is wearing a red shirt, the other a black shirt. They're heading due east."

"Wow!" says one of the tourists. "You can tell all that just by listening to the ground?"

"No!" replies the cowboy. "They just ran over me."

—JOHN GAMBA

As I pulled into the gas station, I noticed a woman trying to push her car toward the pump. Having always considered myself a Good Samaritan, I parked and joined her in pushing her car.

"What are you doing?" she asked.

"I'm giving you a hand," I said. "What are you doing?"

"I'm stretching before my run."

—JIM SHAW

I spent more than two hours in the beauty shop getting my hair permed, cut, and styled. Relieved to be done, I went up to the receptionist to pay. "Good afternoon!" she said cheerfully. "And who's your appointment with today?"

—GCFL.NET

Little Johnny and his friend Tommy were on their very first train ride. A vendor selling concessions came by, and Tommy's mother bought each child a candy bar. Johnny eagerly tore into his just as the train went into a tunnel. When the train emerged, Johnny saw that Tommy was still struggling with the wrapper.

"I wouldn't eat that if I were you," Johnny said to Tommy.

"Why not?" asked Tommy.

"Because I took one bite and went blind for half a minute."

—INNERWORKS PUBLISHING.COM

Today in the markets, helium was up; feathers were down. Paper was stationary. Elevators rose, while escalators continued their slow decline. Mining equipment hit rock bottom. The market for raisins dried up. Coca-Cola fizzled. Balloon prices were inflated. And Scott Tissue reached a new bottom.

—ERIC CAMPBELL

A guy's grandfather clock stopped working. He called a repair shop to get it fixed, but they wanted $50 to come get it.

"I'll bring it to you," the guy said. So he strapped the clock to his back and started walking down the big hill he lived on. Halfway down, he slipped, and he slid down the hill into town just as a lady was crossing the street. He barreled into her and knocked her over. Dazed, disgruntled, and still on the ground, she asked, "Why can't you just wear a wristwatch like everyone else?!"

—ROGER REAKOFF

Groan-Worthy Gags

■

Two guys stole a calendar. They got six months each.
—ALEX DEL BENE

Grandpa always said, "When one door closes, another one opens." Great man, horrible cabinetmaker.
—BUD FRAMPTON

What's the difference between a poorly dressed man on a unicycle and a well-dressed man on a bicycle? Attire.
—GERALD WALL

SHOULD I STOP BRINGING UP MY CAT?

A feline fanatic believes his beloved pet
is truly the cat's meow.

By Jory John

PLACE: A PLAYGROUND

Scene One

LADY: My daughter Lucy said the cutest thing the other day. She was eating some applesauce, and she looked at me and said, "Mommy, how do they get the applesauce out of the apple?"

ME: That's adorable. My cat eats constantly. It's getting a little concerning, honestly.

LADY: Oh. Yes ... I, um ...

ME: He has this meowing routine. He meows from the other room like six times per day. Right? And I just know that when he starts meowing, he's hungry again. And I'm like, "Didn't you just eat?"

LADY: I ... uh ...

ME: But he just keeps meowing, and I just keep feeding him. Mostly just to shut him up.

LADY: I see.

Scene Two

GUY: My son, Nate, took his first step the other day. I'm kicking myself because I didn't manage to film it. What's the point of having all these cameras around if we don't capture these moments?

ME: Oh, wow. My cat, William, has been walking ever since he was born, basically. He's pretty nimble too. He walks on the upstairs banister a lot, and I'm like, "William, be careful!" But he's usually just fine.

GUY: [*Silence*]

ME: Sometimes I watch my cat's feet, the way his paws move. It's really transfixing, you know? I'm sure it's the same with your son.

GUY: You're saying I should watch my son's feet?

ME: [*Not listening, staring at my phone*] You want to see a few videos of William walking around?

GUY: I, uh ... I suppose.

ME: [*Scrolling through more than 2,000 cat videos and photos*] Here, check this one out. Look how beautiful it is when four paws work in tandem, like a fancy watch.

Scene Three

LADY: Not to brag, but my daughter is incredibly bright. The other day, we were in the backyard, and she pointed to a butterfly—

ME: Oh my gosh, my cat absolutely loves butterflies!

LADY: Does he? That's ... great. Anyway, my daughter—Kylie— she looked up and pointed at a butterfly and said, "That used to be a caterpillar, Mommy." I'm not even joking. She's a little genius.

ME: My cat, William, caught a caterpillar once. He chewed on the thing until it was completely mangled, and some legs got stuck to his whiskers. But he was so proud of it, and I wanted to support him, not shame him. Right? So I said, "Good job, William." Even though I was pretty grossed out by the whole thing. I just didn't want to hurt his confidence, you know?

LADY: Well ... [*Pretending to check her watch*] I should really be going ... lots of things on my to-do list today.

ME: William is pretty darned brilliant too. How old is Kylie?

LADY: She's 3.

ME: Yeah, William is definitely as smart as a 3-year-old human.

They're probably about the same level of intelligence right now, my cat and your daughter. Isn't that just amazing?

LADY: That's actually really rude.

Scene Four

LADY: I like to bring my son, William, to this park to get some physical exercise.

ME: [*Stunned silence, my mouth agape, my eyes widened*]

LADY: What is it?

ME: Your son's name is William?

LADY: Yes ... Why?

ME: That's my cat's name!

LADY: Oh. That's, uh ... Wow.

ME: Who was he named after?

LADY: His grandfather.

ME: Same with my cat! His grand-father cat is named William too! He belongs to my cousin. "William the Grandfather," we call him. But he's not as old as a human grandfather. Just as old as a cat grandfather. He's 3—not, like, 70.

LADY: [*Nervous laughter*]

ME: What a day. Two Williams in one park. What are the odds?

LADY: Wait—your cat is here?

A **driver is** really struggling to find a parking space. After 45 frustrating minutes, he begins to pray.

"Lord," he says, "I can't take this any longer. If you open up a space in this lot for me, I swear I'll give up gambling and drinking, and I'll go to church every single Sunday."

Suddenly, the clouds part and the sun shines down on an empty parking spot. Without hesitation, the man says, "Never mind, I found one!"

—IRISHPOST.COM

A **husband and** wife who own a circus walk into an adoption agency looking to adopt a child.

"Are you sure the circus is the best place for a child?" asks the social worker. "I mean, all those dangerous animals, the constant traveling ..."

"The animals are trained," says the wife. "And we have a state-of-the-art 55-foot motor home that is equipped with a large nursery."

"How will you educate your child?"

"We've arranged for a full-time tutor to teach all the regular subjects, as well as Mandarin and computer coding," explains the husband.

"And the nanny is certified in pediatric care, child welfare, and nutrition," the wife adds. The social worker is impressed.

"Well, you do seem perfect. What age were you looking to adopt?"

The husband says, "It doesn't really matter to us, as long as they fit in the cannon."

—PLANET PROCTOR

W **hen my** kid sister and my mother bought three exotic birds, they named them This, That and The Other. After a few months, This died, and they buried the bird in the backyard. A few months later, The Other passed away and they buried it next to This. Then the last bird died.

Mom called my sister and tearfully announced, "Well, I guess that's That."

—GLORIA VITULANO

After our kitten ran up our expensive curtains, snagging them, my wife had him neutered, hoping it would calm him down. A few weeks later, my sister-in-law brought her new boyfriend over to meet us. On the doorstep, she offered him this advice: "Whatever you do, don't touch the curtains."

—JAMES BELL

INSOMNIA JEOPARDY

WAYS IN WHICH PEOPLE HAVE WRONGED ME	STRANGE NOISES	DISEASES I PROBABLY HAVE	MONEY TROUBLES	WHY DID I SAY/DO THAT?	IDEAS FOR A SCREENPLAY
$10	$10	$10	$10	$10	$10
$20	$20	$20	$20	$20	$20
$30	$30	$30	$30	$30	$30
$40	$40	$40	$40	$40	$40
$50	$50	$50	$50	$50	$50

R. Chast

Two aliens land their ship on a golf course and watch a young man play. First, he hits his ball into high grass and mumbles and curses as he goes to retrieve it. Next, he hits it into a sand trap, shouting and swearing on his way to collect it. Then he hits a perfect shot, and the ball goes right into the hole. The first alien turns to the second and says, "Uh-oh—cover your ears. He's going to be really mad now!"

—SWINGBYSWING.COM

"I'm really worried about my dog," Ralph said to the veterinarian. "I dropped some coins on the floor and before I could pick them up, he ate them." The vet advised Ralph to leave his dog at the vet's office overnight.

The next morning, Ralph called to see how his pet was doing. The vet replied, "No change yet."

—MIKE WALT SR.

A customer walks into a pet shop and inquires about buying a goldfish.

"Do you need an aquarium?" asks the salesperson.

"No," says the customer. "I don't care what sign it is."

—FRIARSCLUB.COM

"I'd like to donate my body to comedy."

As a couple who had just moved to a new neighborhood ate breakfast, the wife looked out the window and saw their neighbor hanging clothes to dry.

"That laundry isn't very clean," she said.

Her husband looked but remained silent. For the next month, every time their neighbor hung her clothes to dry, the wife made the same comment. Then one morning, the wife was surprised to see clean wash on the line.

"Look!" she said. "Our neighbor finally learned how to do laundry!"

"Nope," the husband said. "I got up early this morning and cleaned our windows."

—STARTSAT60.COM

I was visiting my sister in Tennessee when we noticed a sign placed by Civil War reenactors that read "Civil War Battle November 6, 10 a.m."

During a poker game at a Florida dog track, a player mentioned that he'd read that the track was the oldest in America. "Do you think that's still the case?" he asked. The dealer replied flatly, "No. They built an older one last year."

—CARLOS DUEFFER

My disappointed sister asked, "Whatever happened to the element of surprise?"

—JAMES METZ

Comedian Mitch Hedberg was eager to hang a map of the world in his house.

"I'm gonna put pins into all the locations I've traveled to," he said. "But first I'm gonna have to travel to the top two corners of the map so it won't fall down."

Talk about a freak accident. My uncle was driving to a hockey game with his two sons when their car hit a low-flying duck.

After absorbing the shock of what had just happened, Uncle Mike

broke the silence with, "Now there's a bird that didn't live up to his name."

—JASON BULBUK

A salesperson stops by to see one of his business customers. Not a soul is in the office except a beagle emptying wastebaskets.

"I'll be finished in a few minutes," the beagle says.

"Incredible!" the man exclaims. "Does your boss know what a prize he has in you? An animal that can talk!"

Alarmed, the beagle drops the wastebasket.

"No, don't tell him!" he pleads. "If he finds out I can talk, he'll make me answer the phones too!"

—BENEFITSPRO.COM

I WAS ON THE BUS THE OTHER DAY AND SAW A GUY SIT DOWN ON HIS GLASSES. I GUESS HINDSIGHT ISN'T 20/20.

—ED POLLACK

I never feel more alone than when I'm trying to put sunscreen on my back.

—JIMMY KIMMEL

There is a light at the end of the tunnel. Hopefully it's not a freight train.

—MARIAH CAREY

Red sky at night, shepherd's delight. Blue sky at night, day.

—TOM PARRY

I hate it when people press the elevator or crosswalk button right after me. You think you press buttons better than I do?

—ISSA RAE

You are only young once, but you can stay immature indefinitely.

—OGDEN NASH

If you're one of those people who says "Please, no gifts on my birthday," you and I are very different. I like gifts. I demand them. I'll make you feel awkward if you don't get me one.

—JOHN KRASINSKI

Start every day with a smile and get it over with.

—W.C. FIELDS

I always wanted to be somebody, but now I realize I should have been more specific.

—LILY TOMLIN

There's never enough time to do all the nothing you want.

—BILL WATTERSON

IF TWO WRONGS DON'T MAKE A RIGHT, TRY THREE.

—LAURENCE PETER

THE GREAT CELERY FLOOD OF 1971

That caper was plum crazy.

By Douglas Wermedal

Celery is dull. To the third-grade mind, it lacks the projectile potential of the pea or the concussion-producing potential of the bulky Brussels sprout. Worse, uneaten celery is almost impossible to hide in a lunchroom.

It was Miss Brewster's job to verify that we'd cleaned our plates, and she required convincing proof before she'd let us go out for recess.

We tried many methods to dispose of the hated vegetable. One solution was to give it to someone else. The Johnson kid tolerated celery well enough, but not on the scale needed to serve the entire third grade. My friend Dan invented the milk carton ruse, which worked for a time—until our friend Rick got sloppy and allowed a few green tendrils to protrude from his carton. Brewster made all of us open our milk cartons, exposing the contraband. No recess.

Later, desperation to get to the monkey bars led me to stuff the celery into my sock. I presented my clean tray to Miss Brewster—and it worked, though we still needed to get rid of the smuggled stalks. Dumping them on the playground wasn't an option; the authorities would hardly miss a heap of moldering celery in the four-square court.

Then we hit on the boys bathroom. Soon every boy was making a pit stop to flush his dose of stringy vegetable.

Unfortunately, we soon realized the downside of what had seemed our perfect crime. The principal announced that the boys restroom would be out of order due to some unusual plumbing problems. Peeking out of the classroom door, we were horrified to see water flooding the entire hallway and janitors frantically mopping the ever-expanding flow.

None of us said a thing, but from then on, we ate every inch of our lunchtime celery ration.

ESSAY CREDITS

CARTOON CREDITS